GOD'S SPECIAL CHILD

— LESSONS FROM NATHAN

and Other Children With Special Needs

by
Donna & Ellis Adee

with
Tom Hunsberger
*Learning Disorders Teacher
National Home Education Speaker
Home Educating Father*

God's Special Child — Lessons from Nathan
Copyright © 1996 by Harvest Publications

First Printing, 1996

Printed in the United States of America

Cover art by Steve Miller and Jan Bell
Page design & layout by C:PROMPT Creations
Hillsboro, Kansas

All rights reserved. No part of this publication may be reproduced in any form or by any means without the prior written permission of the publisher. For information, write to Harvest Publications, 1928 Oxbow Road, Minneapolis, KS 67467.

Library of Congress Catalog Number 96-94761
ISBN 0-9654272-0-X

Foreword

As the former Special Needs Coordinator for Home School Legal Defense I have had the opportunity to talk to hundreds of parents about their special needs children. Although their children's needs range from a slight reading disability to a severe physical and mental disorder, the parents all shared many of the same concerns, problems and questions. For each one of them I often wished I knew a book that I could recommend that could address these issues. Now there is one. I cannot think of one parent who would not have been better informed and more encouraged by reading this book.

Donna and Ellis Adee tutored their son while sending him to the public school so they know what it means to educate a child with special needs. Their own child, Nathan, who is now with the Lord, was the instrument God used to teach them the wisdom and understanding that is found in this book. The word, "Special" is not a clique that Donna has used but rather represents a deep understanding that each of us are created in God's image for a special purpose. Not only does Donna draw on her own experiences, but she also has interviewed countless other parents who share their joys, pains, and wisdom gained in raising children with special needs. Together these parents share a breadth and depth of insight that is priceless for a mother who is just starting the road to home schooling. Let Donna and these other parents cheer you on as you run your race.

> *Therefore we also, since we are surrounded by a great cloud of witnesses, let us lay aside every weight, and the sin which so easily ensnares us, and let us run with endurance the race that is set before us, looking unto Jesus, the author and finisher of our faith, who for the joy that was set before Him endured the cross, despising the shame, and has sat down at the right hand of the throne of God.* Hebrews 12:1-2 (NKJ)

Janet Wayne Walker
Arlington, Virginia

Preface

There are many excellent books published by professional educators on children with special needs but as I checked to see what was available from a parent to other parents from a Biblical viewpoint I could find nothing.

I am a mother and grandmother with a few college hours. My husband and I have had 27 years experience raising Nathan, the youngest of our three children. He was born with a genetic problem called Prader-Willi Syndrome. Since the experts both medically and educationally did not know what to do with Nathan, we had to be our own experts. We had to turn to the Creator, the One who designed Nathan, for the wisdom to raise him and untangle the many physical and educational problems.

If I can share just a few of the many lessons we learned the hard way, my goal to help other parents will be fulfilled. These are lessons that I wish someone would have shared with us in 1965 when Nathan was born. This knowledge would have helped us when there seemed to be no answers. We had to depend on God, who did supply the right information or person to see us through to the next step.

The basis of the whole book is the decision to believe that Christ died for our sins and that we need to ask Him to be our Savior. Both Ellis and I made that decision before we were married. The knowledge that God is in control of everything in our lives, (Romans 8:28-29) and uses it all for our good to shape us to be like Christ is also a vital part of our decisions.

We made many mistakes, there were often difficult times when there seemed to be nothing we could do but my prayer is that in reading this book, you will be kept from making the *same* mistakes and find helpful advice for yourself and the special-needs child that God has given you.

All the Scripture references in the book are from the New King James translation as is this II Corinthians 1:3-4 "Blessed be the God and Father of our Lord Jesus Christ, the Father of all mercies and God of all comfort, who comforts us in all our tribulation that we may be able to comfort those who are troubled with the comfort with which we ourselves are comforted by God." Truly God did give us the knowledge and resources to raise Nathan to be a useful vessel for Him. We wish to share that comfort with those who

are troubled with the care of a special-needs child.
If I can be of further help, please write or call me.

Donna Adee
1928 Oxbow
Minneapolis, Kansas 67467
Ph. 913-392-2750

Acknowledgments

This book developed from being a story about our son, Nathan, who was born with special needs, to being a how-to book for parents of children with special needs. Janet Wayne Walker formerly with Home School Legal Defense in Virginia, gave me the push to write a book to help parents. I had called her seeking a source to contact parents of children with limited mental and physical abilities to interview. After we had talked about the struggles parents go through with their children with special needs, she said, "We need a book to help these parents." That was the encouragement that I needed.

I sent out almost 80 interviews to parents of children with special needs in many parts of the country and in Canada. Kathy Salars of Texas helped by giving me a list of parents to contact, for which I am grateful. Thirty some parents returned the interviews and shared their experiences. Since Nathan our son, graduated from high school in 1985, I wanted input from parents who are currently working with their children both in the public school and home schooling. I want to thank each of you who have taken time from your busy lives to answer my sheet of questions.

These families will be introduced in the first few chapters in detail. In the following chapters I will refer to them by first name and their state. Some requested that I use the names of both husband and wife but all those interviewed are married. The women answered the interview so I have used their names in most of the accounts. Some wished to remain anonymous but wanted me to use their experiences. Our pastor's wife, Verna Matlack, one of those interviewed, critiqued several chapters, and also gave me Tom Hunsberger's name. His help has been invaluable; his encouragement kept me from giving up the whole project.

Tom Hunsberger, who wrote the chapter, "Learning Disorder or Character Deficit" has taken time from his family, busy speaking and teaching schedule to write this chapter. For this I am truly grateful. Tom has worked with special needs children for more than 21 years. His range of experience spans from working with the severe and profoundly handicapped to learning disabled students. He has also taught students identified as Emotionally Disturbed and helped structure vocational training programs for adolescents and young adults with disabilities. He has taught at the elementary, middle and highschool levels as well as working as a Mental Disabilities/Work Study Consultant for several years.

Tom is currently a Learning Disorders teacher at an elementary school in Washington County, Maryland, where he is providing direct services to more than 40 children ages five to ten years. He also serves as the Special Education chairperson for the school, assisting in the identification and diagnosis of children with a myriad of learning disorders. He holds a B.S. degree in Special Education from Clarion State Univ. And a M.Ed in Special Education from Slippery Rock University.

During the past several years, Mr. Hunsberger has been intensely involved in counseling and encouraging home-educators throughout the United States and Canada, especially those who have children with some type of learning disorder. The frequency and demand of this service has increased since he spoke to a large convocation of home educators on the topic of learning disorders during their annual training conference held at the Univ. Of Tennessee in Knoxville in 1994, 95 and 96.

He and his wife, Carol, currently live in Hagerstown, Maryland with their three children, Derek, Shelley, and Erin. They have been home educating for the past eleven years and have been very active in supporting others in their efforts to home-educate their children.

My husband, Ellis, who learned these lessons with me during almost 40 years of married life, has been very supportive and encouraging as I wrote the book. Much of what I have shared has been from lessons we both learned from depending on God and His Word. He struggled writing the 10th chapter because the memories of our mistakes are still with us.

I also want to thank our daughter-in-law, Dr. Shelly Adee, who critiqued the whole book and our daughter, Chris, a home educating mom, who has offered many helpful suggestions. Their honest suggestions helped straighten out my writing. Maxine Johnson, my high school English teacher has critiqued some of the chapters and offered encouraging words. Also Ellen Myers, Sharon Price, Linda Heir, Verna Matlack and Shelly Adee who rechecked every page of the manuscript and marked the mistakes which helped tremendously in the final draft. Nellie and Mary Ann also made corrections.

Most importantly I want to thank God for giving me the ability and love of writing and giving us the gift of a son born with special needs.

CONTENTS

1. Mistakes or Designed by God?........................... 1
   Thank God, He's in Charge
   Should I Get Pregnancy Testing?
   How Do Other Parents Respond to the Birth of a
      Child With Special Needs?

2. Help! My Baby Has Problems!......................... 11
   Major Decisions May Come Early
   To Test or Not to Test?
   Where Do Parents Get Information?
   Do I Tell My Child With Special Needs Everything About Their Problem?

3. Learning Disabilities vs Character Deficits? By Tom Hunsberger.... 23
   A Parent Must Determine the Root Problem
   The Challenge of Requiring Specific Performance
   Does This Child Have a Learning Disorder or a Character Deficit?
   The Challenge for Those Working with the Special-Needs Child
   Four Levels of Root Causes

4. Push or Pamper?....................................... 31
   Special-Needs Children Must Have Consistent Discipline
   Structured or Relaxed Schedule?
   Pampering Never Works

5. Who Will Teach My Special-Needs Child?................. 37
   Teaching Begins at Birth
   Model What You Want your Children to Do and Be
   Control the Inputs

6. Me? Teach My Child?................................... 45
   Parents Have the Responsibility for Educating Their Children
   Why Did You Take Your Child Out of Public School?
   Does Home Schooling Require That Parents Have a Teaching Degree?
   Are Parents Encouraged to Home Educate Children With Special Needs?
   Why Home Educate Your Child With Special Needs?

7. Special Abilities! My Child? 61
    Those Special Abilities May Turn Up Early
    Parents Hold the Key to Unlocking Those Special Abilities

8. Can a Special-Needs Child Respond Spiritually? 69
    Love for God is Not Limited by Mental Ability
    Leadership of the Family is the Husband's Responsibility—God's Principle
    Provide Materials That Will Make Spiritual Training Easy for Your Special-Needs Child

9. How Important Is Socialization? 77
    Children With Special Needs Are Often Not Accepted by Normal Children
    What Is the Real Need for Socialization?
    Children With Special Needs Must Be Taught Correct Social Relationships
    What If Your Child With Special Needs is Severely Handicapped?

10. Guilt or Satisfaction? (Input by husband Ellis Adee) 87
    God's Design for Sex
    Where Is Your Focus?
    Use Caution with Professionals

11. What About Your "Normal" Children? 93
    Recognize That Your Normal Children Have Needs, Too.
    Spend Special Time with the Normal Child
    Teach Your Normal Children About Their Special-Needs Sibling

12. Parents Have Special Needs Also 103
    Cherish Your Wife—Respect Your Husband
    You Must Find Time to Communicate
    Find Stress Relievers
    A Merry Heart Doeth Good Like a Medicine

13. The Future, Where, When & What? 115
    Have a Plan for the Future of Your Special-Need Child
    Set Up a Trust and Guardians for Your Special-Needs Child
    Set Godly Goals for Your Special-Needs Children

14. A Word To the Wise 129
    Parents Never Stop Learning
    Other Parents Have Succeeded with Special-Needs Kids

CHAPTER ONE
Mistake or Designed By God?

Psalm 139:14
"I will praise You, for I am fearfully and wonderfully made; Marvelous are Your Works."

Shortly after the birth of our third child, our family doctor walked dejectedly into my room, "Mrs. Adee your son is not doing well. We are going to move him to pediatrics for some tests." I was devastated. I knew he wasn't responding like our other children had at birth. I wondered how I could be with my son, who might not live, and with our other two children at home. God gave me the resources I desperately needed. He even provided a new Christian friend there in the hospital. God knew that this other mother would be His human instrument.

Thank God, He's In Charge

Alone in my room, I asked God for some word of encouragement. "Please Lord, I need something to cling to with Nathan's life hanging by a thread." In the notes from my daily Bible studies, I found I Thessalonians 5:18 marked, "In everything give thanks; for this is the will of God in Christ Jesus for you." I clung to that verse as a dying man clings to a life preserver. I didn't know if Nathan would live, but I did know that whatever happened was God's will and that I should thank Him.

While Nathan was taken upstairs where I couldn't breast-feed him, this other mother listened, loved, and comforted me in my tears. Somehow I was able to face going home without Nathan. I pumped my milk fully expecting to breast feed him when we brought him home.

That was in 1965. The tests at that time were not as sophisticated as they are today but they did prove one thing: the doctors did not know what was wrong with Nathan. All they knew was that he lay like a limp rag doll without even the energy to cry or suck.

Nathan was lethargic and I kept asking myself if I had done something to cause his weakness? Could it have been the breach birth or his slowness starting to breath? I had so many questions but no answers. The doctors were just as puzzled.

After a week of tests, and before Nathan was allowed to come home, I was visiting our neighbor, a young mother from our church. I told her, "Nathan is going to live, I'm sure of it because God has a special job for him." God had given me a peace about that. This assurance was something I hadn't had at the birth of our other two children. There was no way I could have guessed the special job God had for Nathan, whose name means gift of God.

My mother-in-law was very concerned when she saw Nathan. She had raised eight healthy children and one who contracted polio at eighteen months. She said, "Maybe it was those anti- nausea pills you took those first months." I appreciated her concern, but placing blame didn't help the hurt and frustration of taking care of this weak newborn. He couldn't suck long enough to receive the nourishment he so vitally needed. Nothing worked. She didn't tell me at that time that she didn't expect to see him alive when she arrived home from their three month trip.

One morning at church, an older outspoken grandmother took one look at this weak little baby and said, "You're starving him! Cut a large hole in that bottle nipple and pour it down him." It worked. I would breast feed as long as he could suck and follow with pouring from the bottle. Nathan finally began to gain weight.

Those first weeks and months were difficult. So many decisions and adjustments had to be made. The whole family suffered. I'm sure our other children had no idea why I was spending so much time with this baby. By God's strength and wisdom we made it through that first year.

I know that if Nathan had been born today with his genetic problem and we had chosen to have more children, the doctors would have insisted that I go through all the tests available. I'm not sure if doctors are trying to spare parents from having less than perfect babies or if they are trying to protect themselves from malpractice lawsuits. But when I researched on these tests I found that there can be some troubling consequences from the tests themselves.

Should I get pregnancy testing?

Many doctors are scaring women into all sorts of tests for what some call "a deformed fetus" instead of a baby. To find the latest information on children with disabilities, I checked out a 1992 book from our city library, *Children with Disabilities*, a medical primer by Dr. Mark Batshaw and

Mistake or Designed by God?

Yvonne M Perret.[1] They said,

> Prenatal diagnostic testing is performed to detect a suspected disease; <u>it does not ensure a healthy baby</u>, only one who does not have the disease that the test detects. As prenatal diagnostic tests <u>are not without risk</u>, (my underline) they should be performed only when there is a specific risk and potential benefit.

How can testing be a wise choice in light of Psalms 139:13-14? The Psalmist wrote: "For You have formed my inward parts; You have covered me in my mother's womb. I will praise You, for I am fearfully and wonderfully made; Marvelous are Your works." Our daughter, Chris, delivered her second child with spinal muscular atrophy, a genetically caused problem. Several doctors told them that there was a 25% chance that any other children born could have the same problem. They weren't sure they wanted more children after little Elise died at 8 months. God answered that question for them; He gave them a strong healthy baby boy two years later and a healthy baby girl four years after that. The doctor who had taken care of their dying Elise rejoiced when he delivered that healthy boy.

During her third pregnancy, the doctors offered several tests to check for the genetic problems. Chris said, "I won't have those tests. I wouldn't abort even if they did show a problem, so why should I risk the life of the baby with the tests?" At that time, the tests wouldn't show the spinal muscular atrophy anyway.

One mother of four in Abilene, Kansas, was told by her OB/GYN that her fourth baby should be aborted because he had problems. The doctor (who does many abortions) even called her at home to encourage her to go ahead with the abortion. She refused, and delivered a healthy baby. Doctors and tests are not always correct.

Dr. Batshaw in *Children with Disabilities*[2] wrote,

> Advances in complex technology and the resulting options now available regarding the care of children with disabilities have led to numerous difficult ethical questions. Should screening and prenatal diagnosis be performed on women who are genetically at risk of having children with severe disabilities? If so should their fetuses be aborted? Are there instances in which medical care can ethically be withheld from a newborn infant with a disability? Is it ethical to perform experimental research on children with disabilities? ... Such advocates believe that the fetus is not human until it is able to live independently outside the

mother's womb, generally considered to be after the 24th week of gestation. Prior to that time, a woman should have the right to make a choice as she sees fit.

God assures us in Psalm 139:15-16, "My frame was not hidden from You, when I was made in secret, and skillfully wrought in the lowest parts of the earth. Your eyes saw my substance being yet unformed. And in Your book they all were written. The days fashioned for me, when as yet there were none of them."

Pearl Buck, a famous author, said in her 1965 book, *The Gifts They Bring*,[3]

> One out of every 1000 children born is seriously retarded. Three out of every 1000 are unlikely to progress beyond the mental age of 7 years. Twenty-six out of every 100 are more or less affected so that they are slow of mind.
> What shall we do with these children? They are being born every day. What have we done with them in the past? Until very recently we have done nothing with them, or for them, except hide them. We kept them hidden in homes where they were born, or we put them into institutions because we did not know what to do with them. They created problems we could not solve. We could not answer the unanswerable "Why?" Either for ourselves as a cry out of our own broken hearts, or as questions that others asked. Nor is this entirely changed. Doctors may still advise the parents of an obviously defective newborn child to place him, at once, in an institution.

How Do Other Parents Respond to the Birth With Special Need?

What was your response when you found your child was less than perfect? It is not unusual to go through grieving steps when you find that your child has special problems. Being angry at God, denial or even blaming yourself or your spouse for this child's problems are not unusual responses.

Ellen of Wichita learned right after birth that her seventh child had Downs Syndrome. She recalled, "There was a great sadness when I was told by the doctor that Becky was a Down Syndrome baby."

Fay in South Carolina said, "Our doctor told us that Heather had Down Syndrome a few hours after her birth, but we didn't know 100% for sure until the blood tests came back about two weeks later. She was in the hospital at that time with jaundice when the phone call came to me. Not until the blood tests proved it did I finally accept it. I just believed that it couldn't

Mistake or Designed by God?

happen to our family. We had five other healthy children, why us now? But we loved her from the beginning and decided that no matter what the diagnosis, we would continue to love her because God had given her to us for a reason, and it was our responsibility to accept that and train her the best way we could, along with God's help."

A Wichita mother of a special needs daughter, whose problems didn't show up until several months after birth, expressed concern for parents who go from doctor to doctor to find a cure when there is none. She knew of parents who would go to much expense and effort for a miracle cure. There are unscrupulous people out there who can take advantage of desperate parents. She called them "health and wealth faith healers" who may want your money. She said, "Check with your own doctors before going to any of the special treatments."

Ginia from Maryland tells of having to oppose the doctors when they wanted to stop her from breast feeding her Down's Syndrome baby. Many times a mother can see what is best for the baby. As she and her husband pray about a decision, they may have to say "no" to doctors.

Sometimes a healthy baby can develop a disease or other problem which can cause special needs that have long lasting results. Selena of Kansas delivered a healthy baby, but at 22 months, Stephanie lost her hearing and quit talking. Now, at the age of 14 years, Stephanie still struggles with all schooling and instructions even though she regained her hearing.

Verna of Kansas delivered healthy babies, but when they started to school, she found that two of her five had severe learning problems. This creates trauma for parents who had no idea that there were problems. They often handle the difficulty without knowing where to go for help. That was where we found ourselves so many times with Nathan. When we later did find that he had Prader Willi Syndrome, we were still in a state of confusion; no one knew much about that genetic defect.

Jean of Kansas also didn't realize that her oldest child's unusual play methods were a symptom of many problems he would have with school work. She and her husband, a high school principal, went to several doctors trying to find the cause of their son's problems. It was difficult for her, as a teacher, to accept that God had given them an autistic child.

Janie of Oregon the mother of five, wrote about her three (Phillip, 24; Jon, 16; and Cherish, 8 years) who have various stages of autism. She said,

> *Autism does not affect my children physically. We are a very robust family, but the social and emotional toll on my family could, without the mercies of the Lord, be staggering. Roy and I dedicated all our chil-*

dren to the Lord even before they were born. We knew the child within my womb was a gift of His planning even before we discovered who they were or their handicapping condition. This doesn't mean that acceptance was easy, or that there weren't times of great questioning. (My plan was to have six to eight beautiful, talented, perfectly relating kids. I think I had read <u>Little Men</u>, once too often)

Parents of handicapped children will always run into some step of the grief process on a continuing basis. Every time your child fails to reach a society-expected milestone, physically or emotionally, there will be grief. I guess it came to us when, at school age, neither Phillip, Jon, nor Cherish were able to blend and learn the way parents except of their children. It came when Phillip tried, to no avail, to become a Boy Scout. This grief is normal, natural and to be expected. During the times of grieving, the Lord is your sustainer.

Marsha and Terry from Missouri shared about their only child, Jessica, (now 13) who was born with spina bifida and hydrocephalus. Marsha said,

We knew approximately one hour after her birth. We accepted it immediately and were glad that we were her parents. We were told that she wouldn't live, so we held up the Life Flight helicopter for 45 minutes to make them put a name on her birth certificate, in case she didn't live. She needed to know how important she was to us. The head nurse told us we could put Jessica back in the corner without treatment until she died. We were offended because that wasn't our choice. That was God's choice.

Karen of Kansas who is strongly visually impaired herself, told of Christine, her visually impaired 6-year-old. Christine was born with congenital cataracts on both eyes. She had surgery on both eyes at age 3 weeks, and was fitted with glasses at age 5 weeks. With the surgery and glasses, Christian has visual acuity of 20/100 (normal is 20/20) with no depth perception. Although their oldest child has normal vision, they knew before they had children that there was a 50% chance they could have a child with this problem. Karen said, "Our church was a broad shoulder, especially one family that had a deaf son."

Marilyn of Pennsylvania told about Timothy, 15 years old, who had a pre-natal stroke that affected the whole left side of his body.

It was a great crushing blow and yet in the same hour we knew "God is too wise to make mistakes and too loving to be mean." So we

knew God in His love and wisdom allowed Timothy to have a stroke and He's given us the grace and strength to handle any problems along the way. God has supplied wisdom and strength and when talking about heaven and having a "perfect body" Timothy's response is, "I don't want one, I like it just the way it is."

Jackie of Colorado told of Christopher, the second of their 5 children. He was diagnosed at birth with Golden-Hars Syndrome, which affects the development of the face and head. Christopher's left ear is not fully developed with moderate hearing loss in both ears. The jaw bone on the right side is smaller and he has a restricted tongue. Mental development is slow. Jackie said,

> He was sent home at the age of one week as a failure to thrive until I discovered he was not gaining but losing weight. I took him to a lactation specialist who gave me a special bottle to squeeze the milk into him so he could get milk. His original doctors would have let him die. We've never regretted having Christopher—we know he has a special reason for being in our lives. We have even refused any testing (amniocentesis) to see if any of the younger children would be born with the Golden-Har problem. (It can effect the eyes, kidneys and heart also) Some doctors acted very surprised that we had not rejected our son or his problems.

Nellie of Oklahoma wrote of her 18 year old daughter, C.L., who was born with Elder Dan-los type II, a skin disorder. She had 38 seizures of the grand mal type early in life. At one time, they were told she wouldn't be able to walk, swim, or ride a bike, maybe not even to stand. Nellie said, "She's standing, walking, swimming and riding bike, plus doing very well. Doctors still don't know how she is walking. A wonder, yes, God's little wonder. We had no problem accepting her; she was a gift of God. We loved her so. The news was hard, but we had God."

These special-needs children are not a mistake; they are especially designed by a loving God for His purpose. We may not always feel thankful for this special needs child, this gift from God. If God had asked, we would have said, "No, not me. I can't handle a special needs child." But God, in His omniscient love, gives us an honor when He trusts us with the care of one of His special children.

Several of the mothers I interviewed reported that once they were able to thank God for that child, the child became a wonderful blessing.

I know many times I was not thankful for the problems of raising

Nathan, but I can look back now to see that special purpose of why God gave him to us. As we asked for wisdom from Him to raise Nathan, He gave it to us as He promised in James 1:5. Nathan's problems forced us to depend on the Lord because there were no easy answers. My husband often said, "The older two sort of raised themselves, but Nathan raised us."

Since God is sovereign, nothing comes into our lives without His approval. God doesn't make mistakes; NOR DOES HE CREATE MISTAKES. All His children are especially designed by Him.

A quote that has helped me so much over the years is from Alan Redpath's "Victorious Christian Living." It fits with Romans 8:28-29,

> *There is nothing, no circumstance, no trouble, no testing, that can ever touch me until, first of all it has gone past God and past Christ right through to me. If it has come that far, it has come with a great purpose, which I may not understand at the moment, but as I refuse to become panicky, as I lift up my eyes to Him and accept it as coming from the throne of God for some great purpose of blessing to my own heart, no sorrow will ever disturb me, no trials will ever disarm, no circumstance will cause me to fret—for I shall rest in the joy of what my Lord is! That is the rest of victory.*

Ellen, a Wichita mother of Becky with Down's Syndrome wrote this poem. It describes how God looks at that child He created.

To A Retarded Child

You have a special place
In our Creator's perfect heart and mind.
Beloved little sister! By His grace
You shall appear adorned before His face,
No longer seeming dumb and deaf and blind
Marked by the sin of Adam's fallen kind
In your marred body.
God will find
In you, rejected by this world, a wall
Conceived and fashioned at His glorious call
To bear a silver palace, clean and bright
His stately home and jubilant delight
To men and angels who behold your light
Reflecting His.

> Or you may be His door
> At which our Brother Jesus knocked of yore
> Longing to enter in so one soul more
> In love receiving you might reach repose
> In His new heaven and earth. We will enclose
> With board of cedar, incense—sweet and strong
> This door by which He entered and our song
> Shall praise Him for creating you, forevermore.

"We have a little sister, and she hath no breasts: What shall we do for our sister when she shall be spoken for? If she be a wall, we will build upon her a palace of silver; and if she be a door, we will inclose her with boards of cedar." Song of Solomon 8:8-9

NOTES:

[1] *Children With Disabilities* a Medical Primer by Dr. Mark Batshaw and Yvonne M. Perret, MA MSW, LCSW, Paul H. Brookes Publishing, Baltimore Maryland 21285. 1992 page 23

[2] ibid Batshaw Page 547

[3] *The Gifts They Bring* by Pearl Buck, John Day Company 1965 page 9

CHAPTER TWO
Help! My Baby Has Problems!

James 1:5
"If any of you lacks wisdom, let him ask of God, who gives to all liberally and without reproach."

Parents often face major health problems early in lives of their special needs children. Down's Syndrome children often have heart damage which requires surgery their first year. My husband's cousin spent weeks at the hospital following heart surgery for her four month old son with Down's Syndrome. Friends and relatives helped with the care of the older child at home three hours away. They went through all that only to lose him after months of trying to stabilize him.

That first year was extremely difficult with Nathan. Our day was spent pouring milk down him and exercising him. It was discouraging when he was so slow developing muscle strength. He couldn't hold his head up at 8 months. Chris, our four year old, helped by climbing into his play pen and wrestling with him. My mother-in-law wasn't the only one who was surprised that Nathan lived through his first year. Our family doctor, who had delivered him, called him, "The miracle baby."

Another mother of a Prader Willi son, who is now seven, told of the difficulty in feeding. The hospital wanted her to use a stomach tube which had to be put through his nose. This scared her extremely. Against the doctor's recommendations, she resorted to using a spoon and cup at 3 weeks because he couldn't suck on a bottle. That worked. Often parents know what will work.

Our local doctors did not suggest any special testing for Nathan during his first five years. We knew he was slow developing in such areas as walking and talking but gradually he improved. He was 16 months when he took his first steps while his talking in sentences didn't start until the age of three or four. We never thought of taking Nathan for special testing to find the reason for his poor muscle strength.

Nathan hadn't been in kindergarten long before the teachers were asking, "What is Nathan's problem? We don't know how to work with him. Why don't you take him somewhere for testing?" They had the educational psychologist from the co-op in Salina, Kansas test him after we signed a bunch of papers. They didn't find out much so they also said, "Take him for testing at some research hospital."

Our family doctor made us an appointment at the KU Medical Center in Kansas City, Missouri, four hours away. After two days of testing by professionals, who treated us like we didn't know anything, we were finally ushered into the office of the head neurologist. He announced kindly, "Your son has Prader-Willi syndrome. Just take him home and let him be a happy-go-lucky boy. He won't be able to do much in school. Don't expect him to be able to button a button or zip a zipper." I was in too much shock to argue that Nathan was already doing both those things. We took him home and did what the experts said for a year or so. We let him do what he wanted when he wanted to do it. He did almost nothing in school. *That was a bad mistake.*

There were no books published on Prader-Willi at that time. It wasn't until 1956 that studies were done by Swiss endocrinologists, Prader, Labhart and Willi. We didn't know until Nathan was probably 12 years that Prader-Willi syndrome is caused by a missing piece of the 15th chromosome and is characterized by low birth weight and subsequent failure to thrive, mild mental retardation, severe muscle weakness (hypotonia) and delayed developmental milestones. The next stage reflects almost "thriving too well." A compulsion to eat usually becomes apparent in toddlerhood. Previously agreeable and compliant behaviors give way to stubbornness. Temper tantrums increase in frequency and duration along with a drive to forage and hoard food. Calorie intake requires lifelong external control in order to prevent morbid obesity and its potentially terminal side effects of heart disease and adult onset diabetes. It affects one in 15,000 births. We found out from the school co-op that there were two other Prader-Willi children in our small county. But at that time there was no information or support group. We were on our own. But Nathan's problem taught us to seek wisdom from the Lord often. The experts were puzzled at best and wrong at worst.

Nathan did start gaining weight in junior high and with the weight gain and weak muscles, developed a severe back curve. We took him to several bone specialists to seek the best advice. One told us that if we didn't immediately do surgery, Nathan's heart and lungs would be crushed within a short time. He was ready to call a Wichita hospital to schedule surgery. Ellis said,

"No, we will seek another opinion." The doctor couldn't see why we wouldn't agree. He told us that Crippled Children would pay for the surgery. A county health nurse had shown us what fusing 13 vertebra would involve. We needed more information before putting him through such a drastic surgery.

Since we were flying to California for a family reunion that year, we took Nathan to one of the best orthopedic surgeons at Loma Linda hospital. He told us that if we waited for *years* to do the surgery, there would be no harm to Nathan. But he also said Nathan would have to be in a body cast for almost a year if he had the surgery. Seeking God's wisdom considering surgery to fuse the vertebra, we felt it was not in Nathan's best interest. Instead we chose monthly chiropractic treatments to keep his back flexible. He wasn't in pain and kept active most of the time. He could walk for hours.

Years later, our family doctor told us, "You were wise. They have found that type of surgery doesn't help." Often we had to be our own experts when doctors would give us dire warnings. The God who gave Nathan to us gave us the information we needed to make that decision. We had to depend completely on God for wisdom time after time because the professionals had no answers or their answers were not in line with the wisdom God gave us.

How does a parent decide which medical procedures they should consider for their special-needs child? Naturally, if there are medical procedures that can prolong their life or that give a child a better chance to be independent, a parent should seek the best medical procedure and solicit advice from mature Christian leaders. When we would pray for wisdom God would either provide a person, an informative book or some specific information to help us make that decision.

A book called *Management of Prader-Willi Syndrome* finally came out in 1988, but by then I could have written a book myself. We knew earlier there was a national organization in Illinois and I had contacted them for information. A group of Kansas parents of children with Prader-Willi children started a support group in the 1980s, but they met in the Kansas City area so we were never able to attend. We did take their newsletter and contributed ideas occasionally.

Soon after Nathan started to school, we noticed that following birthday parties, he came home very irritable and could not concentrate on his homework. Our daughter read in the Reader's Digest that children with learning and discipline problems can have greater problems when they eat or drink sugared foods. We took all sweets away and put him on a diabetic diet even before we knew that Prader-Willi children were prone to diabetes. He did much better with his school work and temper tantrums following the removal of sugar. Unfortunately we couldn't keep him from looking for and finding cookies hidden in the bottom of the deep freeze. The school teachers and secretary knew Nathan should not have sugar. When he was in high school, the school secretary would call to report, "Nathan just bought a large supply of cookies from the FHA bake sale." By the time we heard about it, Nathan had already devoured them. He could eat forbidden food faster than anyone I know. I always wondered why they told us when we had no control of Nathan while at school.

Prader-Willi children become very adept at finding forbidden food and some will eat anything and everything. One mother told me that the youngest of her seven children had Prader-Willi and they kept him home until he was 20. He would eat anything that was not locked up, even canned food. She could not take him to the store because he would steal food so quickly that she couldn't stop him. Prader-Willi children become very paranoid about their food. Some will resort to stealing it from neighbors. Nathan only did that once that we knew about. They gain weight on far less calories than the normal person so it becomes a family battle trying to keep the forbidden food hidden. We tried locked boxes, a locked deep freeze and hiding sweets outside the house so our other children could have them. There was no safe place.

Many children with Prader-Willi are put in group homes where all food is kept locked until they are fed. They have ravenous appetites since they never feel satisfied regardless of how much they eat. We wanted Nathan home with us and tried to keep his weight under control. Keeping Nathan from gaining weight was a constant battle. He considered any control of food a lack of love. We considered it *tough love* to take care of his health. Nathan and I had lots of battles over this, especially when I found that he had taken the screws out of the deep freeze padlock and eaten in one night all the cookies and cakes hidden there. I would wake up in the night to hear noise in the kitchen and find Nathan digging in the refrigerator for food after he had eaten a well-balanced meal. I would demand, "Nathan, you get to bed and you stay there." Then I would sleep out in the living room to make sure that he stayed out of the food.

Nathan weighed over 200 pounds by the time he was in high school, which his small bones and tiny feet couldn't carry well. It was like a larger child weighing 400 pounds. Prader-Willi children are short, rarely over 5 feet, so the extra weight was very difficult on his health. *I was beginning to wonder if he would live to accomplish the job that God had for him.*

To Test or Not to Test?

As I interviewed parents, I found that many of them never find the reason or cause for learning problems of their special-needs children. Selena of Kansas knew her 14 year old lost her hearing during that crucial time of 18-22 months when her well developed talking stopped but they never took her for special testing. They didn't feel a need for that. Stephanie never went through the, "Why mommy?" or "What is that, Mommy?" stage which is a vital developmental step for children. She knew when Stephanie was three or four years old that she had problems, but they didn't realize it was long term. They started speech therapy and learned all they could to help her.

Lane, the multiple handicapped 16 year old son of Carol and Lonnie of Kansas, started life six weeks premature. The doctors at Wesley Medical in Wichita, where he was flown right after birth, told his parents, "He has more wrong than right and he will probably be a vegetable all of his life."

It was a very frightening time for them. The doctor left them with the suggestion of institutionalizing Lane. Instead they took him home and loved him. Lane can now take care of his basic needs with the help of hearing aids in both ears, which he received at two years, and strong glasses soon after that. He went through major surgery at the age of eight to put rods in his back to correct the severe spinal curve. With braces he can walk some.

Sharon from British Columbia is another mom who did not realize that her daughter had learning problems. She knew their adopted sons with Down's Syndrome would have problems both physically and mentally but wasn't prepared for her daughter's ADD (Attention Deficit Disorder) problems.

Janice and her husband, of Kansas, had a Down's Syndrome son and then adopted a baby daughter with cerebral palsy. Adapting to two different special needs with no support group or help from anyone has been difficult.

Testing of your special-needs child has to be decided by you, the parent. Well-meaning friends and professionals may push testing but each test, either medical or educational, should be considered by certain criteria: 1) Will this help our child or will it put them under unnecessary stress? 2) If we don't do this test will it prevent us from knowing needed information? 3) Weigh each test individually; one test may accomplish what is needed but the professionals may request many more.

Where Do Parents Get Information?

Selena of Abilene says, "Read everything you can get your hands on about your child's problem." God led her to some excellent books in her local library. One was *Helping Children Overcome Learning Disabilities,* by Jerome Rosner. This gave her information to know better how to work with

Stephanie. Selena also asked many questions from the public school special needs teachers. They have been very helpful even though Stephanie and her sisters are being home schooled now.

A pastor's wife near Kansas City noticed that her second child at the age of 6 months to a year, didn't seem to understand like their older child. She would bang her head on the floor. Their pediatrician was reluctant to agree that there was any problem. Finally at almost three, he began to give credence to her concerns. He sent them to a speech and hearing clinic at a local hospital for evaluation. They concluded that she had the understanding of a 9 month old baby.

Janie in Oregon said that their oldest son was a puzzle to all his teachers. His labels in the public school went from dyslexic to emotionally disturbed and behaviorally dysfunctional, yet he didn't fit all the symptoms. It wasn't until he was a freshman in high school that a discerning teacher realized that his true diagnosis was high functioning autism.

Mary in Indiana has a 20 year old son who was labeled gifted—learning disabled but uneducable. His special needs affect him in every area of learning with speech problems, perceptual hearing problems, visual perception, short term memory difficulties, dyslexia, dysgraphia, discaluia, attention disorder with hyperactivity, asthma and other health problems. He had a twin brother who was stillborn.

Laura of Michigan told of Gideon, the third child of her five. He was born with Williams Syndrome which affects him physically in the form of heart murmur which has to be monitored, poor rotation of his arms and wrists, bad posture, below normal height and a weight gain and mild retardation. At 20 months, after his pediatric cardiologist had checked him, he asked Laura to look at pictures in his huge medical book of children with Williams syndrome. Gideon did have the full lips, high forehead, missing teeth and large eyes. They had to wait another month for the official diagnoses. Laura called the library for information and they sent a few pages from a medical journal. Laura said, "I kept saying, I'm too young to deal with this. I don't know why I said that because I was twenty-five years old at that time. I cried a lot but I also educated myself."

Kathy of Texas found out at birth that their second daughter had Downs. She said,

> The older doctor came into my room and told me that my daughter was mongoloid. I knew what he meant. I was angry that he called Sarah mongoloid in 1985. All the books explained that the name had changed to Down's Syndrome. The sonogram that we had before Sarah's

birth had shown nothing unusual but I believe this was before the days of measuring the skull and leg bones to determine size and growth.

Sandy and her husband of New York adopted a baby girl in 1980 after having five children of their own. This baby was born with an encephelocele (sack on the back of her head.) It was removed the day after birth, along with 1/3 of her brain, leaving her totally blind, profoundly retarded and later diagnosed with cerebral palsy. She said,

> When the social worker asked us to take Sarah we hesitated since neither of us had any family or friends with any noticeable handicaps and we didn't have any training for such a severely disabled child. They assured us it would only be for two weeks and we finally agreed. Obviously there were many turns of events. We adopted Sarah the following year and have always know in our hearts that it was what God had planned all along.

Sheila of North Carolina wrote of her two special-needs children, Katye who is eight and Huxley who is six. Katye has epilepsy with seizures. Sheila said,

> She processes things differently in her brain. When Katye was four, I took her to the doctor because she was having night seizures and constantly wetting her pants during the day. The doctor didn't believe me about the night seizures. I stood my ground and to the doctor's dismay insisted on further testing. After an EEG, a different doctor, who had never seen Katye called us and matter-of-factly told us, "Katye has epilepsy." No other explanation. We were in shock. Later that day a nurse called and scheduled a MRI brain scan. When I asked why, she said, "To rule out a brain tumor" More shock and now panic set in. No one talked to us or answered any questions until we met with her neurologist. Finally he answered all our questions and calmed a lot of our fears. With phenobarbital her seizures are controlled.

Sheila continued, "Her neurologist told us that her type of epilepsy indicated that she would be a genius in one specific area and we have found that one to be art. She is very gifted artistically *but* she only draws in black and white. She can't understand colors yet."

Sheila's other child with special needs is Huxley, who had the same genetic problem associated with the liver and lungs as his father. As long as he isn't having allergy or asthma problems he learns well, but when he has health problems we just shut down school."

Mary Ann of Kansas noticed her youngest son in seventh grade had not learned to read or write. He had been labeled ADHD (Attention Deficit Hyperkinesis Disability) with coordination problems at the age of seven. The school had sent him to a doctor for the diagnosis. He was on Ritalin for about three years but his father did not agree on medication so he was off it in the summers and not on it at all in fifth and sixth grades. The teachers in the public school wanted him on Ritalin. He was only one of her five that she home educated.

Valerie of Massachusetts told of Megan, her eight year old, with Down's Syndrome. Because of this she is mentally retarded. Her skills are scattered and she functions at the 3-4 year old level with some skills below that. She does not have any medical problems such as heart trouble but she has low muscle tone and Atlanto-axial instability. Valerie said, "When the doctor first told me about Megan I started crying because I was just so shocked. I never expected this to happen to us. The doctor left to do tests on her. I really do feel God chose Megan for us."

A mother in Maryland has a sixteen year old son who is labeled ADHD with short-term auditory memory deficits, weakness in receptive and expressive language, disparity in visual-perceptual speed functioning and dyslexia. She said, "We investigated everything we could find, including types of special education, reading books on the disabilities, going to many doctors and specialists and getting information from other parents."

Cindy from Kansas knew there was something wrong with Randon, her second son but it wasn't until he was four years old that a doctor finally said, "He has Prader-Willi syndrome." This doctor became very interested and did research to find more about Prader-Willi and how to work with Randon.

Debbie, a special education teacher from Kansas, said that the youngest of her three was "labeled with degrees of autism???" (Misdiagnosed) and placed in Learning Disabilities in the public school. She said, "I think that he was 'border-line gifted-LD,' Travis never talked much before the age of six; he could but just didn't. He was in his own little world most of the time."

Terry and Robert of Maryland wrote about Stephen, almost nine, their youngest son who was born with Down's Syndrome. He had the Atrial Septal Defect but it closed up without surgery. Mentally he is high functioning. They adopted him knowing that he had Down's Syndrome.

Linda and Phil of Minnesota told of adopting a son with special needs after having three daughters of their own.

> Very early in this journey of adopting a special-needs son, we realized that only the Lord, who led us into this commitment, would be able to sustain us through it, for each in our family has discovered that we did not fully realize the impact that mental retardation would have on our lives. We have found the Lord to be faithful, but we have also had to learn to be even more patient, flexible and creative than we were."

Evelyn, of Kansas (a special-education teacher) became aware that one of her twin daughters (now 24 years) had difficulty learning when she was in 2nd grade. "I suggested to the teacher that perhaps she should be tested; then I was unable to accept the results. The school psychologist helped me accept the fact that Kari did have a learning problem."

As I read the interviews from each of the parents, I could see that at first the shock of having a child with special needs was almost overwhelming but as God began to show them how to care for this child He had given them, they began to see that it wasn't an impossible situation. As they applied Biblical principles to raising this child, the child became a joy to their family as well as to others.

Do I Tell My Child with Special Needs Everything about Their Problem?

Nathan started being tested by the school psychologist and at the KU Medical center by the time he was six. The Medical Center wanted us to come back the next year but we refused. We could see no benefit from more testing. All the testing created anxiety for him and us because they probed into our personal lives and his. By the time he was in junior high, Nathan wanted to know what these school reports and doctor's reports contained. Usually we allowed him to read them. To forbid him from reading the reports would have created more anxiety for him. If we had it to do over again, we probably would not put him through all those tests. Many were not beneficial, especially the ones at the mental health clinic.

We know that at times Nathan used his physical and mental problems to his advantage. I will share later in the chapter on schooling how this became especially obvious there.

Remind A Special-Needs Child That God Designed Him

I wish that we had reminded Nathan often that God created him just the way God wanted him and that God had a special job for him. We did not do this. I'm sure that we made him feel inferior because of the constant battles over his eating. EVERY SPECIAL-NEEDS CHILD SHOULD BE

REMINDED OFTEN THAT THEY ARE CREATED BY GOD JUST THE WAY HE WANTED THEM.

There is no simple way to raise a child with special needs. It takes unselfish commitment on the part of the parents. We parents are the ones who have to make the final decisions on medical and educational intervention.

The professionals may or may not be correct, so each decision has to be seriously considered. God provides the wisdom and resources as we seek it from Him. I had to remind myself often of the verse that God showed me when Nathan was born: I Thessalonians 5:18 "In everything give thanks; for this is the will of God in Christ Jesus for you." If we parents see this child as designed by a loving God, the child will learn to accept and thrive with his special need and become a vessel God can use.

Helps for Parents of Special-Needs Children

Prader-Willi Syndrome Assoc. headquarters at 2510 S. Brentwood Blvd., Suite 220, St Louis, Missouri 63144, Phone 800-926-4797

For Down's Syndrome: The Michael Fund #721, 400 Penn Center Blvd., Pittsburg, Pennsylvania 15235

A group that helps churches mainstream students with disabilities in Sunday School, VBS and worship services is: Christian Church Foundation for the Handicapped (CCFH). Write Dr. Jim Pierson, P.O. Box 6869, Knoxville, Tennessee 37940, Phone 615-579-0883; fax requests 616-579-0942

Most other SN problems also have a national headquarters for information.

Another good resource for all special needs is: *NATHHAN Magazine*, 5383 Alpine Road SE, Olalla Washington 98359. Phone or fax 206-857-4257. They publish a quarterly magazine to encourage, inform, educate and provide resources for home-educating children with special needs. They suggest $25 for a one year membership which gives you use of their lending library.

JAF Ministries (Joni and Friends) has a monthly newsletter accelerating Christian ministry in the disability community. Their address is P.O. Box 3333, Agoura Hills, CA 91301. Phone: 818-707-5664; Fax 818-707-2391; TDD: 818-707-9709; E-Mail: 102704.3130@compuserve.com

Resource Material for Special-Needs Children:

Selena Book of Abilene, Kansas supplied this list. She said that she would be glad to talk to any parent. Her address is: 1019 2000 Ave., Abilene, Kansas 67410. Phone: 913-263-7545

Help! My Baby Has Problems! 21

Turnabout Children by Mary MacCracken (very good)

A Parents Guide to Learning Disabilities by Johanna Fisher (very good)

Helping Children Overcome Learning Disabilities by Jerome Rosner (Selena's favorite)

Preparing for Adolescence by James Dobson (very good)

Parenting Isn't for Cowards by James Dobson (very good)

Learners-Slow by Peter Bell

Home is a Learning Place by Helen Ginandes Weiss

Verbal Learning and Retention by John Fry Hall

Learning by Doing by Carlos Clinton Crawford

Montessori: Prescription for Children by Reginald Calvert Orem

Human Characteristics and School Learning by Benjamin Samuel Bloom

How Children Learn by John Holt

RIF Guide to Encouraging Young Readers by Reading is Fundamental

Underachievers by Benjamin Fine

On Helping the Dyslexic Child by T.R. Miles

Basic Teaching for Slow Learners by Peter Ball

CHAPTER THREE
Learning Disorders vs Character Deficits

by Tom Hunsberger

Philippians 4:13
"I can do all things
through Christ
who strengthens me."

A Note From Donna :

Tom Hunsberger has excellent experience working with children of all ages who have special needs, after teaching twenty one years in the public school. He has learned from experience that he, as a teacher, cannot meet all the educational needs of these chidren. With his large caseload of over 40 children, without an aide or para-professional, it is impossible to implement ideas thta he knows would work. That is why he tells parents how to work with their children.

His knowledge on how to find the root problem comes from Biblical principles which were also the guiding principles in educating our son. Once Tom learned that we shared the same goals, he agreed to write a chapter for the book. This chapter is part of the material that he has shared for three years at the Advanced Training Institute International Seminar in Knoxville. Read this material carefully and thoughtfully.

A Parent Must Determine the Root Problem

For those of us who have had the privilege to work with special-needs children for any length of time, the question has sooner or later arisen regarding aptitude verses attitude. Simply put, if the child is unable to accomplish or master a task with which they are being presented, is it a matter of can not or will not? Is the child simply unable to perform the task or achieve the goal because God has not empowered him with the ability or is he not at that developmental stage required to undertake mastery, or does he simply not want to do it? Is he truly drawing upon all his God given abilities to achieve his maximum level of performance by demonstrating such character qualities as endurance, perseverance, diligence and thoroughness, or is he just merely trying to "get by" through manipulating the situation and those involved, giving them the perception that he is unable to perform the task which is being requested of him?

Although this is not the easiest of questions to answer or situation to discern, it is essential that the parents and other individuals working with the child determine from which root the problem stems. If the child is to continue development and growth that is commensurate with his ability which will allow him to become all that God desires him to be, the issue of aptitude or attitude must be confronted and discerned so that he may fulfill God's purpose for his life. In order that he may fulfill God's purpose for his life, the parent must know if the problem comes from an issue of aptitude or of attitudes and the child's training and educational program must reflect this. The methodology one would implement in dealing with a problem of understanding and ability would be completely different than that utilized when encountering an attitude or character deficit. Many children have not been allowed to experience the fulfillment of their spiritual and mental capabilities because their growth has been stunted by loving, caring, dedicated, well-meaning parents and others who were functioning under the misconception that the child's lack of achievement and behavior was arising from a limited aptitude rather than the true source which was a wrong attitude and deficiencies in character.

We need to remember that our purpose in life is not to garner fame and fortune or attain high levels of intellectual prowess, but to bring glory and honor to our God and Creator. Our heavenly Father, who wants only the best for His children, including all those with special needs and disorders, desires that we achieve all He has designed for us to be. This can only be accomplished by developing Godly character which will provide the foundation for our learning and eventually fulfilling the purpose He has for us. It is this principle that impels us to realize the necessity and crucial nature of developing positive character within each of these special children and forces us to confront the aptitude versus attitude dilemma.

As children of our Heavenly Father, we each have within us, the ability to attain a life of Godliness and to be conformed to the image of His Son. This promise is not limited to those at or above a specific level of intellectual ability or those without the "noticeable" flaws, deficiencies, and disorders which most special-needs children possess and exhibit. This is a promise to all those who are His. It is based on the knowledge of this promise that we must approach the character training of all special-needs children.

The importance of character training cannot be overemphasized, especially when dealing with those special-needs children who are more cognizant of their environment and capable of higher level interaction with those they encounter on a day-to-day basis. This population of special-needs children are more capable of implementing and manifesting their own self-will and attempt to do what we all want to do—controlling our own lives rather than submit to the authorities God has placed over us.

The Challenge of Requiring Specific Performance

With this understanding firmly in place, we are now aware of the challenge that lies in the path of each of us who encounters the special-needs child in the relationship where we are requiring of them specific performance. This could be as complicated or demanding as writing a short paragraph informing someone of how they spent their summer vacation or as simple as picking up a piece of paper and placing it in the wastebasket. We must continually be alert to the child's understanding of the process of the task and their attitude towards it. Is this activity beyond their current limits of ability or are they manifesting a lack of a character quality necessary to fulfill the request to the best of their ability? Are they being attentive to your instruction or request or are they demonstrating unconcern towards your words and desires? Are they approaching the task with diligence or are they simply attempting to see the job through to completion applying minimal effort? Are they obediently and joyfully attending to the task presented or are they carrying out the task grudgingly, quietly desiring to fulfill their own agenda?

The attitude or mind-set with which one approaches a task has a far greater effect not only on how the assignment is executed, but also the quality of the end result. This is especially true for the special-needs child. Because of their disorder or disability, many of the tasks which, for us, are simple and even mundane, can be, for them, an enormous challenge posing significant hurdles. Consequently, it is critical that these children possess, to the optimum, all the positive, Godly character which can be instilled with them so they will be capable of performing all tasks until the Lord calls them home.

Does This Child Have a Learning Disorder or a Character Deficit?

To gain a deeper understanding of the relationship between aptitude and attitude or how a learning disorder can either be magnified by a character deficit or actually be rooted in a character deficiency, let's examine in a cursory manner learning disorders and how one might discern where the "root" of the problem lies. For if one gains an understanding of this process, the task of separating an aptitude from an attitude and character deficits becomes somewhat simpler.

Learning is defined as acquisition of knowledge and/or understanding of something or the acquiring of a skill through study, instruction, or experience. A disorder is the disturbance in the normal function of something. Consequently, a learning disorder can be explained as an impairment in any learning channel whether input, processing, or output that interferes with learning and can vary in severity. Therefore, we will first examine the various levels a disorder can manifest and how an individual can cause a disorder to increase to a greater level of severity through either character deficits or placing themselves in an area or situation which God never intended for them. Then we will explore the process of tracing a disorder to its causal factor. Even though the situations and examples which will be shared are broad and general and are intended to focus our attention on special-needs children, the concepts and principles which they illustrate are applicable to us all.

A learning disorder can occur and disrupt the normal function of various bodily functions, such as physical, mental, or sensory. Someone with cerebral palsy would have a disorder that would be categorized into the physical realm while an individual with limited intellectual capabilities would be diagnosed as having a disorder in the mental domain. And an individual suffering from partial or total color blindness could be considered to have a sensory impairment. The disorder in each of these areas can also vary in the degree of severity.

The least of the severity levels would be the deficit level. At this level, one would experience a slight lacking in some necessary quality or element that would cause a minor disruption creating the inability to perform up to "normal" standards when performing a task or acquiring a skill. Someone with cerebral palsy in which one side of the body was slightly involved would be lacking in the normal motor coordination required to drive an automobile. This is not to say that they would not drive. It merely infers that the task of driving would be somewhat more difficult for them than for an individual who is not afflicted with this disorder. An individual with a slight deficit in mental ability might experience difficulty with various daily living skills such as balancing a check book or reading a technical manual to assist them in the repair of an appliance. Again, this is not to say that they couldn't accomplish these tasks. It merely states that the deficit would cause the task to be somewhat more difficult for them than for an individual with unimpaired mental ability. And the one with the impaired color vision may experience difficulty with the color coordination of his clothes as a result of his deficit.

The next level of severity is that of the handicap. A handicap is a disadvantage that makes achievement unusually difficult but still not impossible.

However, the task is more difficult to achieve than at the prior deficit level. The same individual with cerebral palsy who only encountered a slight problem learning how to drive an automobile will discover that attaining their private pilot's license and flying a small aircraft presents a greater challenge—making achievement of this goal far more difficult. The person with the limited mental ability who chooses to become a semi-skilled tradesman will probably discover this outcome to be somewhat more difficult than balancing his checkbook. And the person with the impaired color vision would find becoming a chalk artist a greater challenge to overcome than simply coordinating his clothes. Consequently, even though their impairments or disorders did not change, because of the activity selected, their disorder could be classified as a handicap rather than the less severe deficit classification.

The most severe of these three levels is that of a disability. This infers that the individual is unable to pursue an occupation or course of action as a result of a specific disorder. In other words, an individual would not be able to pursue or participate in an activity because the nature of his disorder would not allow it. The person with cerebral palsy, although he may have been able to learn to drive an automobile and fly a small aircraft would not be able to become a brick mason. This occupation would make demands on him that could not be met as a result of his disorder. And the individual with the limited mental ability who was, with some amount of difficulty, able to balance his checkbook and become a semi-skilled tradesman would be unable to become an electrical engineer, since the disorder he possessed made this occupation unable to be pursued. Likewise, the person with the impairment in color vision would be disabled if he attempted to become a computer technician.

Although the disorder or impairment did not change or vary in each of these individuals, the situation in which they were placed or the course of action they chose to pursue dictated the severity of their disorder.

Special-needs children encounter these situations on a day-to-day basis. Even though their impairments may not vary, the nature of the situations and the demands of various tasks can cause a fluctuation in the severity level of this disorder. Consequently, at times they may only be mildly challenged; frequently, the activity will require a greater testing of their ability, and occasionally they will be unable to pursue or become involved in an activity because the demands it makes far exceed what their impairment will allow.

The Challenge for Those Working with the Special-Needs Child

The determining issue and challenge for those working with the special-needs child is being able to discern the level of severity being created for the child by the current situation or circumstances, The old adage, "No Pain, No Gain," is as applicable in the life of the special- needs child as it is in ours. If they are allowed to remain in their "comfort zone," their growth will be hampered and their opportunities limited and their usability for the Lord significantly diminished. Their disorder urgently insists that character be in the forefront of their training so that their disorder will not become a millstone around their neck. But instead it should be a tool used by God to conform them to the image of His Son, Jesus Christ that they may attain the greatest that God intended for them. Always remember, special people have a special purpose.

Deficits in character can influence the severity of a disorder in the same manner as situation and circumstances. However, their effects are far more devastating because they influence all areas in the life of the special-needs child while situation and circumstances are usually temporal and specific. As long as positive, Godly character is in place within the child, he will be able to overcome his circumstances and grow through various encounters he experiences. Unfortunately, if the child is not of good character, he will be overcome by his circumstances. Searching out the root cause to surface problems is essential for anyone working with the special-needs child, for it's at the root of the problem that the cure must be applied. If you merely deal with the surface issues, the problems will never be resolved since they emanate from the roots and frequently a conduct or character disorder can be masked by a surface problem that appears to be a valid learning disorder. And when the legitimate learning disorder does exist, it is frequently exasperated be an underlying character deficit.

The Four Levels of Root Causes

There are four levels which must be examined when searching for root causes. The first is that of the surface problems. These are visible qualities or actions which present themselves as viable problems that are creating various obstacles in the child's life. The second level is identified as surface causes which appear to be the source from which the surface problem emanates. The third level is distinguished as root problems. These problems are not as easily identified as those at the first two levels and consequently left unprobed and undiagnosed. The fourth and most critical level is that of the root cause. It is at this level that the problem originates. If the disorder is not traced to this level, it cannot be properly remediated.

To aid in the understanding of the process involved in searching out the root causes of learning disorders, I will utilize two very common problems encountered when dealing with academic performance in special-needs chil-

Learning Disorders vs Character Deficits

dren. I will first explain the surface problem with its accompanying surface cause. Then I will shift my attention to the root problem and root cause.

A problem frequently encountered by those working with special-needs children is that of the difficulty of following verbal instructions. This would be identified as the surface problem. The next step in resolving this disorder would be to seek out the surface cause, and it is normally at this point, the surface cause, that probing for the origin would cease; whether or not an acceptable diagnosis was determined. This particular surface problem could have as a surface cause a deficit in auditory memory. This would be a sensible answer since anyone would have difficulty following verbal directions if they were unable to retain the directions long enough to carry them out. However, other factors can create a problem with following verbal directions. One such a factor could be that the child was not demonstrating the character quality of availability which is making one's schedule and priorities secondary to the wishes of those in authority over you. If the child was not demonstrating this character quality he would be manifesting self-centeredness and would not be interested in what those who were speaking to him were saying. Therefore, this character deficit could appear as a valid learning disorder. If the child possessed a slight deficit in auditory memory, the disorder would appear even more severe.

In delving into the root problem and root cause, we could identify two possibilities in each area. The problem, if it were true auditory memory weakness, would be located in the area of auditory processing and the root cause would be found in God's design in that God allowed this problem to be present so that He could carry out a special purpose. However, if the surface cause was that of the child being self-centered and not demonstrating the character quality of availability, the root problem would be a conduct disorder while the root cause would be a character disorder.

Another surface problem commonly identified in special-needs children is that of being a poor reader. A surface cause for this could be a weakness in short or long term visual memory. This would make it difficult for the child to retain the visual picture of words and create reading difficulties. Yet, there are frequently other causes that can manifest themselves as a reading disorder that are not valid learning disorders. A common cause for poor reading is that the child is not thorough. In other words, he is not attending to the various factors in the reading process. This will diminish his effectiveness and he will be incomplete in what he is doing. This character deficit could appear as a legitimate learning disorder. And if the child has even a slight reading problem, the absence of good character could intensify the disorder into a magnitude that would allow the child to be classified as having a learning disorder in reading.

Again the root problem and cause could be two-fold. If the surface problem was located in the area of visual memory, the root problem would be a processing disorder and the root cause would be in God's design for the child. But if the surface cause was found to be in the area of a lack of thoroughness, the root problem would then be that of a conduct disorder with the root cause being one of character.

A myriad of problems could be circumvented if we would focus on the character of the child as well as understand how to search out the root causes of the surface problems he is manifesting. All too often we only complicate the child's life and increase the severity of his disorder when, through misdirected loving intentions we allow ungodly, negative character to dwell within the child, damaging his spirit and hindering him from fulfilling God's design and purpose.

CHAPTER FOUR
Push or Pamper

Proverbs 29:15
"The rod and reproof give wisdom,
but a child left to himself
brings shame to his mother."

Special-needs children must have consistent discipline

The experts at Kansas University Medical center encouraged us to allow Nathan to do as he wished. Phyllis, my teaching sister-in-law, who had tested him at six years said, "You must discipline him. Any teacher will work with a special-needs child if he is disciplined but if he is not, no one can help him."

There is a tendency for parents of children who have mental and physical problems to pamper them. Often professionals tell the parents to be lenient. If there are other children in the family, they may be required to protect the special-needs child and to do his chores. If this is encouraged without the special-needs child learning discipline, they learn to demand extraordinary privileges to the detriment of themselves and the family.

My husband was raised in a family of nine children. His second oldest brother contracted polio at the age of eighteen months which resulted in a severely curved back and one leg shorter than the other. His parents spent much of their short supply of money, time, and effort trying to get this handicapped son's physical problems helped. But they neglected to take care of a very special need: discipline. Being one of the smartest in the family, this brother soon learned to use his handicap to his advantage. He would start fights at school and his brothers would have to defend him. He was babied by his father and catered to by his mother. Physically, as an adult, he could run heavy equipment and do almost everything the other brothers could but he lacked the discipline to stay with a job or a relationship. If it didn't please him, he would walk away without a word of explanation.

Once we were made aware that Nathan could and should be expected to do his school work, clean his room and small chores, we realized he had acquired the "talent" of avoiding doing what was asked. Since he fell asleep almost every time he sat down, it was easy to forget that he wasn't doing his school work or his chores. We had to undo the mistake we had made in allowing him to do nothing. After we found that Nathan had learned very little by the end of second grade, we decided that we needed to get involved in his schooling. We found that he hadn't been *told* that he couldn't do the work but between his sleeping and unwillingness to do the work, they had allowed him to do almost nothing. From then on we *told* Nathan to bring home anything he did not finish at school. Nathan would bring it home and Ellis, who has more patience than I do, would spend 30 minutes convincing him that he was going to do the work. Nathan had learned to use his handicap to his advantage. His screaming, "I can't do it, I'm tired, or I don't want to do it" became so bad some nights, that I shut myself in the far bedroom. I couldn't stand to listen, but Ellis would stay with him until he did it. That might take hours. If they didn't finish at night, they would work in the morning. We had to undo the mistakes of several years and it was not easy.

Nathan, at eight years, started his own style of showing his dislike for the circumstances or rules. He would run away. The first time he was angry with his sister he ran down our country road towards the neighbors over a mile away. We should have spanked or disciplined strongly then, but he was so shaken up at the time that we didn't. We were soon to regret the lack of discipline.

Later that same week, we were at an out-of-town football game with our oldest son. We left Nathan and Chrissy with a teenage girl. In the late evening, the baby-sitter had told him and Chrissy to come inside to take baths for bedtime. Nathan didn't want to take a bath so he refused to come in with the girls. They went back for him but couldn't find him anywhere on the farm. They called my parents, who lived on a nearby farm, and other neighbors to help look for him. After looking for an hour or more, they called the sheriff to help look. Our neighbor put in a call to the school where we were attending the game but we had already left for home.

It was a moonless, very dark night. Nathan still had not been found when the sheriff's deputy came flying over the hills at 85 miles per hour to help look for him. He almost ran over Nathan, who came out of the pasture a mile from home covered with mud and without shoes. The next day, Nathan showed us where he had walked near deep gullies and ponds. He almost cried about not finding his shoes. He had walked over three miles in total darkness and hadn't been scared. Again we did nothing except scold him. He seemed truly sorry. We thought that would be the end of his running away. Running away became Nathan's escape when he was fed up with parents or problems. Usually once or twice a month, he would disappear. At first we would frantically look for him, but seldom could we find him. An hour or two later he would come home. He usually walked a mile or two from home. I feel that our lack of consistent Biblical discipline in this area was a bad mistake. We would not have allowed running away by our other children. Why should we expect less from Nathan? The medical professionals told us not to expect much and we thought that they were the experts, but God's Book makes no exception with a handicapped child. Hebrews 12:6-7 "For whom the Lord loves, He chastens, and scourges every son whom He receives. If you endure chastening, God deals with you as with sons; for what son is there whom a father does not chasten." Every child is different regarding discipline. What works for one child may not work for the other. Once you find what works, be consistent. This is especially necessary for the special-needs child.

Other parents shared what they had found with their special-needs children. Jean, of Kansas, a kindergarten teacher and mother of an autistic son said, "I have learned from my teaching that most children do not know how to sit and listen to someone teach. They would learn in church, but many don't go to church. The best teacher in the world with the best of teaching won't be able to help a child who hasn't learned to listen." She felt that allowing children to watch television by the hour was not preparing the child for learning. Children need to be conversing with their parents or hearing books read.

Verna, another Kansas mother, said of her two sons with learning problems, "I don't treat these sons any different than the other three children. I expect them to do what the others do. I push to the upper limit. There is a fine line between pushing for them to make progress or so hard that you frustrate them, but they should not be babied."

Structured or relaxed schedule?

Nathan liked a routine. Changes upset him. Normal children are usually flexible but Nathan didn't adjust to changes easily. Once he decided on a certain way of doing things, it was a real battle to get him to change. He started telling us early in his life that he had to have a bright light in his bedroom because he couldn't wake up to go to the bathroom without it. His older brother, whose room was across the hall, was not happy with the arrangement but with the door shut they could get along.

When we traveled, Nathan had to take that same lamp because the home where we were to stay might not have one. This routine became his practice for the rest of his life.

He developed diabetes at age 20, which forced us into a meal routine.

He had to eat at the same time every day. Being farmers, we were often eating the evening meal at 9 or 10 p.m. during the busy summer season. This wouldn't work with Nathan. He made sure that we served it at 6 or soon after. He had diabetes as well as his Prader-willi problem to use as leverage. Finally we adjusted our evening meal to 6 if Ellis was working near home.

One funny routine that Nathan chose was putting baby oil in his nose because it became dry and would bleed. I suggested, "Nathan, I don't think it is good for you to use that all the time."

Nathan responded, "I have to have it." He was using almost a bottle a week because he usually spilled much down the drain every time he put some on his finger. It took the doctor to finally convince him that it was not a good practice.

Structure and a consistent life-style give security to the special needs child. A regular routine with a consistent time for meals, sleeping, etc. goes a long way to build self-control in the child. If they know that meals will be served at a certain time, that they are expected to be in bed at a definite time and every day they have chores to perform, they can build on that settled life-style. But if, on the other hand, food is eaten any time all day without the routine of a family sitting down together, thanking the Lord for the food and spending time sharing their day, the child never learns the self discipline of routine. All children thrive on a schedule but especially the child with special needs.

Jean of Kansas said, "It is hard to have a structured life-style with four boys under eight years and one who is autistic, but it really helps. We try to be as structured as we can."

A pastor's wife near Kansas City said, "Our twelve year old daughter who functions at the level of a two or four year old, demands a very structured life-style and consistent discipline."

Carol of Kansas, the mother of multiple-handicapped Lane, (now 16) says of structured life-style and consistent discipline:

> *Definitely! With having done 16 years of day care and watching many different parents' techniques, I am still amazed when parents feel they are doing their child a favor by being permissive with them. Structure and consistent discipline are key foundations for every child. Without them, they flounder around and feel insecure. Lane has never required much discipline, but from the time he was young, I felt that no matter what else he could learn in life at least people did not have to dread being around him due to his behavior. I am so thankful that I was able to implement that, even though it was very difficult at first*

because he had been through so much pain and discomfort with multiple surgeries, that it was emotionally tough to be firm with him. I have had others tell me over the years how pleasant it is to be around Lane. And even with his limited amount of understanding, he is my most polite to remember his manners. I feel strongly about this issue and could go on and on."

Pampering Never Works

Proverbs has some excellent verses on discipline. One that is very pointed is 29:15, "The rod and reproof give wisdom, but a child left to himself brings shame to his mother." (17) "Correct your son and he will give you rest." Yes, he will be a delight to your soul. I'm convinced that often my lack of *consistent* discipline caused Nathan much grief. Sometimes it is easier to just ignore problems or to over-react to accidents or immaturity.

As a mother, I know that in my impatience with Nathan, I often yelled rather than took him by the hand to help him carry out a request. He was constantly trying the limits, and being our youngest, I kept trying to fit him into the mold of his older brother and sister. Bathroom training was one of the hardest areas because he was almost ready to start school before he had that completely under control.

Nathan may have caused us problems at home but in public he was well behaved; in fact many people did not know that he had a learning problem. With much effort and discipline, we taught him that when adults were talking, he was not to constantly interrupt. *I knew that if Nathan was going to fulfill the special job that God had for him, that he would have to learn discipline.* Some areas we did well in, while in others we didn't stay consistent.

We have been in homes where the child (not always with special needs) constantly interrupted so that conversation was almost impossible. One of our friends had a son who was struggling in public school because he talked constantly and interrupted everyone. They removed him from the public school and home educated him. Within a few months, his constant talking became more normal and he learned to control his actions until it was a joy to visit them. The special attention from his parents with more consistent discipline took away his habit of interrupting.

Tough love requires the parents, regardless of how mentally or physically impaired their child, *to make discipline a must* and that the discipline should be in the consistent pattern that God has set forth. *Proverbs* 6:20-23 says, "My son, keep your father's command, and do not forsake the law of your mother. Bind them continually upon your heart. Tie them around your neck. When you roam they will lead you; when you sleep, they will keep you; and when you awake they will speak with you." Ephesians 6:4 gives some cautions: "And you, fathers, do not provoke your children to wrath but bring them up in the training and admonition of the Lord."

Finding that fine line of consistent discipline with a special-needs child may take more time, effort, and prayer, but the far reaching results will be blessings in the years to come, and the special-needs child will have the security of knowing that you love them enough to discipline them. Children can sense when a parent treats another child differently. A friend shared that a Christian family had told about a foster son they had in their home. One day the little boy crawled into his foster dad's lap and asked, "How come you don't love me like your other children?" He father said, "But I do love you." The little boy said, "Then why don't you spank me like you do your other children?" The father had to tell him that the social services would not allow him to spank.

Because we feel sorry for the child who has so much difficulty mentally and physically, we tend to give in their demands. The earlier we start consistent discipline, the better prepared the child will be for life and accepting authority from other adults and for making decisions on his own. No matter how severe the handicap, a loving parent has to stand firm on discipline. To not do so will handicap the child in many more ways.

I told our children that God says in the Bible that if a parent loves a child he will spank them. They didn't agree or really understand that concept when I sent them out for a little green branch from the plum tree to use on the seat of learning. (I learned of the green switch from a Christian sheriff. He said, "It stings like all get out but doesn't damage the skin.) They learned that disobedience has consequences but reaped the result of being able to go from complete dependence to independence. A child who has not learned obedience from a parent will not be able to move into the obedience of God. A parent is given the responsibility of preparing that special-needs child for the significant purpose God has chosen for him.

Consistent Biblical discipline in a structured home situation promotes a secure environment for all children but especially the special-needs child.

CHAPTER FIVE
Who Will Teach My Special-Needs Child?

> *Deuteronomy 6:6-7*
> *And these words which I command you today shall be in your heart; you shall teach them diligently to your children and shall talk of them when you sit in your house, when you walk by the way, when you lie down and when you rise up."*

Teaching Begins at Birth

A young mother of a special-needs child asked me, "Who is responsible for schooling my child? Is it the government, the state or the parents? I really don't know who." As soon as I hung up the phone the words from Deuteronomy six came to me. I wrote back to Jean to share those truths with her.

God has made us parents responsible for teaching our children. There is no one who will love them as much, or care as much as we parents. As Lana, a home school mother from Salina, Kansas stated, "You are teaching your children from the minute they are born. Schooling doesn't start when they are five. You have been teaching all the time."

Ray Wenger, of North Carolina, a home school father of eight, told in a family seminar that a baby will have Bible verses learned by the time he is able to talk if you quote verses to him at every diaper change. It seems like we miss so many opportunities to teach—while we sit in doctor's offices, drive to town or church, or give baths, etc. Gloria Gaither and Shirley Dobson have written an excellent book to help parents on teaching Bible concepts. *Let's Hide the Word* is an excellent resource.[1]

Model What You Want Your Children to Do and Be

When our children were in their teens, Ellis said, "I wish someone had told me years ago that our children would become what we are. *Our children model after us.*" If we are critical, they become critical of others; if we have a great sense of humor they also will learn to laugh; if we take them to church rather than send them, they will model that also. It is frightening, the responsibility that God gives us parents as we teach, train and raise that child from complete dependence to complete independence.

Nathan remembered everything he heard, even my telephone conversations which I didn't know he had overheard. Weeks later, he would ask embarrassing questions about something I had forgotten. So often I would hear the children criticizing someone and would scold them. "But Mom, that is what you said." The modeling goes on when we least think we are teaching and is absorbed in small bits over time.

We have never *told* our children to study the Bible. Ellis and I read the Bible on our own each day. Sometimes we read it together as a family. We tried various methods of family devotions but Ellis liked the spur-of-the moment times with the children. One would crawl into bed with him to hear a Bible story while I finished evening housework. Soon that became their special time together where all three would be tucked in with him. Sometimes the request would be, "Tell me about when you were a little boy," stories or even, "Tell me about when Grandpa Ben was a boy." Since the Adees have always been excellent story tellers and never seem to forget details, these stories became more exciting with every telling.

We had a game board and several games we played as family but often Nathan couldn't do these so reading worked much better. The one game we could all play was UNO; Ellis who hates card games, would play that.

Since teaching begins the minute a child is born, the parent has been given much responsibility to mold and train that child. The special-needs child may require more time in the training but the principles are the same: "Train up a child in the way he should go and when he is old, he will not depart from it." Our most effective teaching is the day-to-day modeling. They need to see our faith in action, that our belief works in our daily lives.

Since it has been several years since I have had young children, I asked the mothers I interviewed how they worked with their special-needs children. Rosalie, mother of seven in eastern Kansas, told of the birth of her youngest, almost 4 years ago, "When Harmony was born, the doctor said he wasn't sure, but he thought she might have Down's Syndrome. When I looked at her face, I could tell right away that she did have Down's Syndrome. It didn't matter, for we loved her before she was born and our whole family rejoiced in her birth just as we would have that of a normal child. Harmony was and is a much-loved and much-wanted baby."

Rosalie told of her daily routine with her daughter:

Frequently Harmony helps me bake bread. We count cups of flour. Sometimes as I measure ingredients, I let her pour them into the bowl.

I let her knead her own tiny loaf of bread. She loves to work with the dough and it teaches a sequence of commands that can be applied to other skills; "Push it down;" "turn it around;" or "fold over." When the dough is put to rise, I clean up the cabinet and Harmony washes her own highchair to remove the spilled flour.

We are doing pre-curriculum training right now, things such as learning obedience, counting things; learning to draw "o" and "i"; learning colors; playing with math manipulatives; listening to stories; "playing" the piano, toy tambourine and cymbals; learning to dress herself; helping with household chores, such as rinsing dishes, folding washclothes, setting the table, taking papers to the wastebasket and sweeping (Harmony has her own toy broom that she uses only when I use mine.)

Valerie from Massachusetts said she had thought about home schooling since Megan was a little over two but they were strongly discouraged by her Early Intervention therapist. This advice kept them from making that decision for several years. "We didn't think it was legal to teach your own child with special needs, and we didn't think we were *able* to do it because of her disability."

Valerie put Megan in public school kindergarten but was seeing undesirable behaviors coming out in her which were not acceptable. Valerie said,

The public schools are so worldly in what they teach. We don't have anything to do with Santa or the Easter Bunny; we celebrate Christmas and Easter for what they are. We focus on the spiritual aspects of those holidays. But at school they really push Santa and the Easter Bunny, they spend weeks beforehand reading books about them and doing projects and art work with them in it. While we are trying to help Megan understand that Christmas is Jesus' birthday and Easter, His resurrection, her school is telling her Christmas is when Santa comes and Easter is when a rabbit hides eggs. It's like we worked so hard to teach her the truth and they were just undoing it all!

Cindy of Kansas learned helpful ideas for their son from the hospital infant stimulation program from birth through three years. The hospital tested and worked out a program of helps in the physical, occupational and speech area during three sessions each month. They gave suggestions like putting bells on his shoes to help him learn to walk. At 3-5 years, Randon went four mornings a week to Kid's Connection in Salina which is a part of the public school system. Cindy said, "This gave him a lot of social opportunities that he hadn't had before."

Terry and Robert from Maryland adopted Stephan at 6 months, knowing that he had Down's Syndrome. They had been home schooling their other two sons. Terry said, "The adoption agency board approved us for adopting Stephen and even commented that the fact that we home schooled was one of the plus factors in their approval of us. They felt that our other children would not be exposing him to as many viruses while he was young and that when he reached school age they felt that one-on-one tutoring was still a better type of education than sending him to school."

Ellen of Wichita told of Becky, her 25 year old daughter with Downs. "When Becky was little, a friend, who is a professional psychologist/counselor and educator, told me, 'Becky will learn nothing new after the age of 12.' She is still learning; the expert was wrong."

During the time we had worked night and day with Nathan on his studies, the educational psychologist at school told us, "My testing shows that he has improved so much but it is just because you worked with him."

I asked, "Couldn't other parents do the same?" He didn't seem to think that they could or would. That is a shame, because I've seen some special-needs children who could have learned to read if someone had worked with them one-on-one. Why aren't parents committed to preparing that child to handle life by teaching them how to read? Phyllis Schlafly says that a parent or grandparent can teach a child to read with short sessions each evening. Her *First Reader*[2] is a new and better phonics system especially designed to teach young children to read at home. She says to teach them before they start to public school or they will become confused with the look-say method.

Our minds retain everything we see and hear much like a tape recorder so we found that with our children and especially Nathan, we needed to control the inputs.

Control the Inputs

Both sets of grandparents offered us their extra television sets, beautiful floor models. Ellis said, "Thank you but no thanks." He could see how quickly our children and he became addicted to television when we visited Grandpa and Grandma. We also noticed that the programs affected them adversely. Instead, we chose to make reading our family program. We joined book clubs and when the books arrived, we read them as a family. One of our favorites was Dr. Seuss' *Green Eggs and Ham*. Ellis could read these with great drama and excitement and the kids loved it. I remember once receiving a new Dr. Seuss book only to have the electricity go off that night. We read it by the gas light as we all sat close together near the lamp. Some of Dr. Seuss' books don't offer the best teaching for children but most are fun reading.

Another excellent addition to our family entertainment and knowledge was a set of 40 dramatized Old Testament records.[3] Nathan was only a few years old when they started arriving two at a time every month. He would listen to the records by the hour. He remembered everything he heard and in Sunday school, he could answer questions when the other kids (and some adults) didn't have a clue. Nathan had problems with counting change or doing math but when it came to Bible stories, he knew the answers.

Our small town library was a place we visited often. All our family were, and still are, avid readers. When Nathan learned to read in second grade, nothing could stop him when he wanted to research something. He loved history and would research on a certain person or time. The Czars of Russia and Anastasia excited him. He would march into the library during grade school years and ask, "Do you have anything on the Czars of Russia?" The librarian would look at this chubby boy and say something about, "Nothing in children's books." Nathan would insist, "Then give me the adult books." His bed was usually covered with books. His reading was slow and his comprehension not up to normal but once he understood, he didn't forget.

Nathan couldn't hold back his excitement when he found that Anastasia, daughter of a Russian Czar, was related to Prince Philip of England. He said to me, "I'm going to write to Prince Philip and tell him that he needs to take care of her cause she never got back any of their jewels when they killed her parents." He painstakingly typed a letter to Prince Philip. I was sure there would be no response but after several weeks an airmail monogrammed letter arrived from Captain James Fraser of Buckingham Palace saying: "Dear Mr. Adee. The Duke of Edinburgh has asked me to thank you for your letter. The contents of which have been noted." (It was dated May 12, 1988) We framed that letter for Nathan.

Since Nathan was not allowed to purchase candy treats, he started buying books. We encouraged him to use the library but he still wanted to own the book himself. He begged to buy a book every time we went to town so we said, "You may buy one a month." He still had a huge library of biographies, historical books as well as Christian fiction.

Another subject Nathan liked to research was China and the Chinese Emperors. His brother, who was in college, started bringing home international students several of whom were from mainland China. Nathan, who was in high school then, would quiz them by the hour and remember their answers. The next time they or other Chinese students came to our home, he had more questions to add to his information. Thankfully, the Chinese know more about their history than Americans do. Nathan purchased many books about China. He would check at used book stores and library sales as well as buy new. The Chinese were impressed with his shelf of Chinese books and music tapes. *I was almost sure that God's special job for Nathan would be in historical research or helping in a library.*

We didn't tell our children to read. We read to them, listened to them read and made quality books available to them. All of our family are readers; our older two prefer to read rather than watch television now that they have their own families.

Music is another technique which develops so many areas in the special-needs child. Ellen of Wichita said about Becky, "I sing Christian songs with her almost every day to keep up her repertoire. She has a remarkable memory for songs, people's names, faces (even after not seeing them for years) and locations."

Carol of Kansas told about Lane, who has many mental and physical disabilities, "We discovered about 4-5 years ago that Lane has perfect pitch when it comes to music. He has always loved listening to music and responded to the beat at an early age, but while I was playing the piano one day, he matched the ending note on his keyboard."

From the time Nathan was able to walk, he would bounce to music. Grandpa Adee said, "Donna has a dancing boy." At 14 months he was making sounds like singing in his bed even though he didn't talk until much after that. He sang *Jesus Loves Me* while I played the piano when he was 18 months. Music appreciation is not limited to mental ability like other abilities.

Since Nathan was in Sunday school every Sunday from the time he was a baby, he soon picked up the Sunday school songs. Before he could say his own name, he could sing the words of 8 or 10 Sunday school songs.

We purchased records of quality music for the family. There are so many choices available now, some especially for children. Just lately, I babysat with a young neighbor girl who had her own set of Christian song cassette tapes. She would listen and sing as she played with her dolls.

Our family wasn't blessed with singing talent but that didn't keep us from singing together. We often gathered around the piano and sang hymns and gospel songs. Ellis, who says he can't carry a tune, sang along with us. We belted out gospel songs like, *On the Jericho Road* and *Battle Hymn of the Republic.* Nathan could sing quite well but unfortunately later in life his asthma problems kept him from singing. Following one of his sick spells, he asked to sing *Because He Lives.* I regret that we didn't allow him to sing that Sunday.

Other parents shared how they worked with their children at home. Jane in Oregon told about their second son, Jon:

> He was classified by the public school as trainable, mentally handicapped. The diagnosis was Cerebral Palsy as he has unusually limp muscle tone. While living in California he went to a special school which took him to see the A's baseball team. Later he was given some baseball cards at school for good behavior. I was doing dishes one day and Jon came up to me and started reading!
> "Mom, is that Harmon Kilabrew?" Jonathan proceeded to read all the baseball cards and not from the visual clues as the face or uniform. We tried all sorts of tricks to test him and he passed them all. Sure enough, in his secret self, his autistic spirt, Jonathan knew how to read and it wasn't just "Dick and Jane" either.

Karen from southern Kansas, who is legally blind, sends her visually impaired daughter to the public school. She said:

> I have worked with the school system and insisted they give me things to do at home. I read a lot to my children when they were preschoolers, talked a little about phonics, pointed to words as I read the books aloud and read words when they occurred in our everyday life. Early someone gave me this advice on raising a visually impaired child: "talk, talk, talk." I explain everything I am doing to Christine, including pointing out words, explaining why I do what I do and show how I use reading as part of our everyday life. We believe reading is an escape for her because she can't see distance well. It is an outlet, a window on her world.

These parents have discerned like we did, that most of a child's learning comes from the home. As our children model our reading, quality music, and daily lessons in attitudes and actions, we give them a strong foundation for life. God has given us that responsibility as well as the resources to accomplish it using His Biblical principles.

NOTES:

[1] *Let's Hide the Word* Gloria Gaither and Shirley Dobson. Published by Word Publishing, Dallas, TX 1994. This can be purchased from any Christian bookstore in paperback.

[2] *First Reader System, Inc.* P.O. Box 495 Alton, Illinois 62002. Phone 618-462-8622. Orders and Inquiries 800-700-5228. There are other readers using the phonics method. This is one with which I am familiar.

[3] Dramatized Bible stories can be ordered from Bible in Living Sound, Box 234, Nordland, Washington 98358. Phone: 1-800-634-0234, Pacific time 9-5. They are called, *The Bible In Living Sound*. They are now on cassette tapes.

CHAPTER SIX
Me? Teach My Child?

> *Proverbs 22:6*
> *"Train up a child*
> *in the way he should go*
> *and when he is old*
> *he will not depart from it."*

Parents Have the Responsibility for Educating Their Children

When he was five, Nathan had more learning problems than we realized. We depended on the professionals in the educational field to show us what to do. With the knowledge that we have learned in the last few years, we would have educated Nathan completely differently. Hopefully, our mistakes will help other parents of special-needs children.

We thought Nathan could handle first grade at the age of six especially in our local village school, the last country school in the county. Since Lawrence Pacey, who had 13 children of his own, was an excellent teacher for our older son and daughter, we knew he would be patient with Nathan. With 21 children in grades 1-6, they were one big family. The village school at Wells, Kansas was almost like a large home school. The whole community revolved around the school events. The two room school was packed for the annual Christmas program and the last day of school potluck dinners.

Mr. Pacey made learning fun. Math was practiced by ciphering on the blackboard, English was put into practical work by writing letters to any student who was sick, thanking anyone who helped the school or spoke to the students. Crafts were learned as a reward for school work finished. Students could choose from many assorted wood working projects from making bowling pin lamps, wooden turtle shaped foot stools to sanding boards. Recesses were special events for making rope from binding twine or playing softball with Mr. Pacey actively involved.

Nathan would have been accepted even though he couldn't do all that a first grade child should do in handwork and he would have learned by listening, his special talent. Nathan loved to visit school with his brother and sister. We didn't know until this year that the school principal, in town, told Mr. Pacey not to allow Nathan to visit. Mr. Pacey not only let him visit but had the older girls read to him. He was part of the "family." The kids accepted him because he was the little brother of Eric and Chrissy.

We regret that we chose to send Nathan to the kindergarten in town. There was no kindergarten at Wells. The testing that Phyllis, my teaching sister-in-law, did convinced her and in turn us, that he couldn't do the writing required of first graders.

Nathan's entrance to the school in town brought as many problems as it did help. The stress of hurrying him to leave on the bus each morning was just one of the problems. One morning he was hurrying to brush his teeth preparing to leave. Instead of toothpaste, he grabbed the Infra Rub for sore muscles. After much spitting and sputtering, he was ready to leave for another day at school.

Once at school they didn't know how to work with him and insisted that we start testing by the educational psychologist. The testing didn't give much help so that was the time they encouraged us to find the medical reason for Nathan's learning problems. We took him to the Kansas University Medical Center in Kansas City as soon as we could obtain an appointment.

Somehow he made it through kindergarten, but the teacher recommended that he stay in kindergarten for another year while the educational psychologist wanted him in the L.D. (Learning Disabilities) classroom. We were sure the professionals knew more about helping Nathan than we did so we signed the papers. Most of the class of ten were mentally retarded or had behavior problems. Nathan soon began to pick up their negative attitudes and actions. The teacher tried to teach the class, but with such varied educational problems and only one teacher, it was impossible. Educationally Nathan did almost nothing that year. It wasn't the teacher's fault, she tried.

Selena of Kansas is another mother who tried the public school with her Stephanie, whose problems seemed to start from a hearing loss at 18 months. She said:

> Stephanie was in a learning resource room from the first grade up; she received special help with speech and certain classes up to three hours a day. She was mainstreamed the rest of the day. When she was 10 years old, we started considering home schooling. I checked it out for one year to learn all I could. Stephanie had the same special education teacher for four years. Then when Abilene went to attendance centers, Stephanie was in a larger class with a different teacher. That year we started home schooling, she would have been one of 17 students with only one teacher

plus one aid. Two of the members of the class had behavior disorders. We felt it was not a positive learning environment for Stephanie. Parents who keep their special-needs children in the public school need to observe their child's class and question teachers. The teacher may be forced to do group teaching with a large class so that the IEP (Individual Educational Plan) can not be fulfilled for each child. It is not fair to the child because they are in the class to work with their area of exceptional needs which may not be the same as the other children. It is not usually the fault of the teacher; they are limited by the system. One teacher can't handle that many. The teacher is frustrated also.

At the end of Nathan's year in L.D., the educational psychologist told us that they were moving the class to Salina, twenty-five miles from our home. They wanted us to sign papers for this plan. We could see no benefit from the class or from Nathan riding the bus an extra 30 minutes each way, so we refused. They were quick to tell us that we were making a bad mistake. (A few years ago we learned that schools receive extra funding for each special-education student.) Ellis had to strongly insist, even to the point of saying we would go to court, to keep Nathan in Minneapolis.

We mainstreamed Nathan through the first and second grade with some remedial classes. He didn't do much in class but through the help of one special-education teacher, himself handicapped with cerebral palsy, Nathan learned to read. Another special-education teacher wasn't as helpful. The first grade teacher assumed he was receiving his lessons from the special education teacher so she didn't work much in the regular classroom with him. It was several months before Nathan told us that the special education teacher was not well focused in class. Upon checking, we found that she had a night job along with her special-education classes. Even though Nathan wasn't being taught, we still left him in her class.

At the end of second grade, it became obvious that Nathan was not learning his subjects. Before school started the next fall, we met with his teacher, a young energetic lady. After explaining all of Nathan's problems, we assured her that anything Nathan did not accomplish in the classroom, we wanted him to bring home. With her help and our tutoring he did learn that year for probably three reasons: 1) His parents became involved, 2) His maturity level had developed to where he was ready to learn, 3) He had a teacher who spent much time and effort working with him.

Neither my husband nor I have college degrees but in order for Nathan to accomplish anything in the public school, we started tutoring him every morning, evening, weekend and summer. Since the school day was very tiring for Nathan he slept on the bus traveling home. Traveling on the bus was another aggravation for Nathan, the kids teased him unmercifully. I'm sure his sleeping prevented him from hearing some of it.

Once convinced that he had to do his home work, Nathan would fall asleep in the middle of a problem. If a birthday had been celebrated at school with cookies and Koolaid, he would be so hyper from the sugar that he couldn't do his studies that evening. Ellis spent hours every evening convincing Nathan that he had to do his school work. After three years of doing almost nothing in school, he didn't want to work. Nathan could do most of the work orally but not the writing or at the speed required at school.

We wish someone had told us about home education at that time. It would have been many times easier than sending him to public school and tutoring him. *It also would have allowed us to better prepare Nathan for the special job that God had for him.* It also would have relieved much of the stress on the whole family. Not only could we have chosen the curriculum to fit Nathan's specific needs but we could have adapted it to his type of learning and physical stamina. Nathan was an auditory learner while the public school is set up for visual and writing skills. There was no way Nathan could handle all the writing required even when the teachers cut the amount drastically. Our local teachers really tried to meet Nathan's educational needs but they were limited by the system. They were as frustrated as we were.

Maxine Johnson, Nathan's sixth grade teacher (as well as English teacher for Ellis, myself and our two older children) tested Nathan for a case study for the college class she was taking. She wrote this about his educational abilities at that time:

> *The reading problem appears to reflect a developmentally delayed learner. Nathan is limited in mental maturity and has difficulty in accepting and/or completing an assignment without considerable supervision. Since his previous teachers have realized Nathan's physical problems, they have been kind and helpful to his academic performances. It is natural that he is protected at school, at home, perhaps over-protected.*
>
> *As a result, Nathan is slow, sometimes unwilling, to take much initiative with his written work and reading assignments. He does not follow directions unless given one-on-one teacher help. His writing is difficult to decipher.*

That one-on-one help was really what he needed.

She suggested that he learn typing which he did learn in high school and became quite proficient at it. But even that ability didn't give him the speed to be able to prepare all the written assignments required.

Janice of Kansas who tried the public school and didn't like her son being labeled, is home educating their 13 year old son with Downs Syndrome and younger daughter with cerebral palsy. She said:

> Home schooling allows the parents to capitalize on what the child can do and patiently await the skills he has yet to master. This could never happen in a public school environment. People still have such strong stereotypes of special needs children. Doctors and educators actually frighten parents by indicating that they must have special knowledge (to educate their children), but parents know the best and really are the best teachers. That's what the Bible teaches too.
>
> I don't have a degree but my college studies were in early childhood education. You would think that would be great background, however, it didn't include any special education courses. So most of what I learned really didn't prove beneficial for working with my children.

Janice shared that Lucas is reading up with his age level which is rare for Down's children. Janice said, "I use unit studies for the most part. Our desire is not just education but also to help them develop Godly character. So, the unit studies we used are based on specific character traits we want to emphasize and develop: respect, obedience, love, loyalty, patience, etc.

Laura of Michigan wrote:

> I always knew I would home school my children. None of them have been in public school or private schools. Of course, the doctors told me to call the local school district and get all the services I could for free. Gideon needed P.T. (Physical therapy) O.T. (Occupational therapy) and speech for sure they said. My first call was to Home School Legal Defense Assoc.[1] They advised me against informing my school district. When we started, home education was illegal in Michigan. We were labeled "underground" home schoolers. I couldn't risk exposing our school. We opted to keep Gideon off the special education lists. (Home education is now legal for all reasons in Michigan. For a while it was just for religious reasons.)

Verna another mother of Kansas said:

> I started home schooling when our oldest was in the second grade. Nathan, our second, was in public school kindergarten and enjoyed every minute but learned absolutely nothing. If we had been smart we

would have started home schooling at the kindergarten level for him. Instead we started him with first grade material. We would get him up at 6 a.m. to drill him, we didn't know any better, we just kept telling him. "You can do this," it was a real struggle but he finally could do it. It started getting easier for Nathan by the time he was in Junior high. We probably prolonged the problems by forcing him. Nathan's problem was that he was not ready for formal teaching. Home school leaders disagree about this but I think you have to take into account the individual child, like the Bible says, "train up a child in the way he should go"—<u>which means lead him in the way he is individually bent</u>. They can't be stuffed into a certain mold.

Both of Verna's sons with learning problems have blossomed with home education as have their other three children. At fourteen and eighteen, Jon and Nathan have developed into exceptional young men. They can converse with adults easily and naturally, when hired to do yard or farm work, they do quality work and they can give an articulate stand for Biblical principles even when their peers disagree. I know because I have watched their development for over seven years.

Other parents who have achieved success from home education are Marsha and Terry of Missouri. They wrote:

After spending five years doing everything we could to prepare Jessica (now 13) for public school, she had orthopedic surgery right before kindergarten. That surgery meant that she wasn't walking adequately on her own and would need assistance. The school officials were not receptive to her need for assistance and were not planning to educate her. Their plan was to push her through without challenging her academically.

At that point a Christian friend, who is a public school teacher, adamantly suggested that we enroll her in Calvert Home Instruction, which we decided to do. Jessica has progressed and succeeded so well that the doctors and surgeons in Omha recommend home education to other patients' families as an educational option.

Janie of Oregon told about her three autistic children:

Both my sons were in the school system before the home school movement took root. Our normal daughter blossomed in our Christian school in New Mexico where we were living at that time so I expected Philip to do the same. It was one of those grieving times again as his misunderstanding of social clues and other learning difficulties caused his dismissal from the Christian school there. So I purchased <u>A Beka</u> home school materials and taught both children at home. This was no mean feat as I had both a toddler underfoot and an infant while home was temporarily a twenty-three foot motor home.

All three of Janie's autistic children have learned to read once she unlocked their particular learning styles. That is the blessing of working with children at home, the parents can seek out and work with the special learning problems of their child.

Nellie, of Oklahoma, mother of 18 year old C.L. said:

> *Some friends got us started into home schooling. May God bless them for that. Yes, a teacher felt that home school would help C.L. but I knew if it would help that child, it would and could help our normal child as well. When C.L. went to public school, we worked every day for four to six hours but they just weren't teaching her and they said so also. The school just wasn't giving her the education we both wanted for her. After home schooling, C.L. did so much better than in public school. She has graduated from home school high school getting a certified diploma.*

Some of the parents I interviewed have kept their children in public school. Evelyn of Kansas who trained to be a special education teacher after her children were in school said:

> *School was very difficult. Kari and her dad did homework every night. John had the patience of Job and was able to actually 'teach' Kari concepts she didn't get at school. However, this created a problem as homework was done correctly. John couldn't understand why a teacher would want Kari to do the homework wrong and not learn. The teachers couldn't understand why, if Kari did the homework, she did so poorly on tests. We had many meetings. The school psychologist helped the teachers to understand that we were trying to help her. Kari did learn to read very well.*

Jean of Kansas, whose eight year old son is high level autistic, has requested that a para-professional work with him four hours a day in the public school where she teaches. She says, "We asked specifically to have a para-professional with him every day." Not every child receives that kind of special help in the public school.

Cindy of Kansas, whose seven year old Randon, has Prader Willi syndrome like our Nathan, mainstreams in the public school and they too requested a para-professional to be shared by their son and one other special needs child. Both Jean and Cindy live in small towns with a small public school system. They are both actively involved in the learning of their children.

Carol of Kansas said about her 16 year old son:

> *School has been an interesting challenge each time we move. I would say that probably each system was meeting Lane's education needs adequately within time but some needed a little more prompting to do so. We have moved quite a few times with my husband's career (school counselor) changes, so we have faced this same scenario several times. Lane's needs may be more unique than some children's and he needs quite a lot of one-on-one in the classroom so this has presented problems at times. It has been made clear to me that it is so important to have a well-written IEP so that you can use it as your tool to show others that your child does have needs in these specific areas. This has probably been one of our greatest helps. I do not have any great expertise in writing IEPs but with knowing what Lane's needs were and what I wanted him to accomplish, the staff people competently wrote those into the necessary goals. Trial and error is a great teacher. Also we learned over the years how to best word something or some small detail to add for clarity. There is no way to tell another parent exactly what worked with him, except to stay aware of the classroom—visit when possible, ask a lot of questions (yes, even those dumb ones) and look for the progress that should be there even if slight.*

Carol said that Lane is now able to read a few survival words like "men" and "women," "exit" and "stop" and "go."

Karen of Kansas who is legally blind said:

> *I never saw home schooling as an option. I would have liked to home school but had school personnel and resources available to me. Even though I am also visually impaired, I felt inadequate to know how to help our daughter, Christine and yearned for the advice from others. My sister has been a big help because her son is visually impaired also and she did home school her children.*

Why Did You Take Your Child Out of Public School?

Denise, of Kansas, who has a master's degree in special education with an emphasis on learning disabilities, has a 13 year old autistic son whom she has home schooled since 1991. She said,

> Jesus told me that my children would love to have fun with me; that they wanted to spend time with me. Deuteromony 4:10 says the parents may teach their children and Proverbs 22:6 says "train up a child in the way he should go; and when he is old, he will not depart from it."
>
> During this time my husband, Paul, was taking a class on home schooling and the benefits of it. I told him if we had a computer, I would home school. Also, at this time (1991), our school district was using the PALS curriculum which stands for Positive Alternative Life. This meant bisexuality, homosexuality, transsexuality and heterosexuality were all positive alternative lifestyles. Also, birth control methods were discussed which included abortion but not abstinence. Monday of that week, we bought a computer, Wednesday that same week Paul pulled the kids out of PALS. I still wasn't sure we should home school. However, the Lord kept working with my heart through different means. I was concerned about our finances. A friend said, "If God wants you to homeschool, He will provide the finances," "Seek ye first the kingdom of God and His righteousness and all these things shall be added unto you." (Matthew 6:33)
>
> Later that evening I was listening to a Christian kids program and the whole message was on Matthew 6:33. The next morning I was driving to work at the public school and the song on the radio was, <u>Seek Ye First</u>. I thought, "God, are you trying to tell me something—like home schooling my kids?" This was the first step—a giant step of <u>faith</u> it was and still is.
>
> The Lord God is truly an all-knowing God. Alleluia!! I majored in education in college then went on to get a master's degree in Special education with emphasis in learning disabilities. The background in special-ed definitely prepared me for teaching my special education kids in the public school This was just one more helpful step in preparing me for teaching my own children.

Cynthia of Maryland tells about her son, with problems from ADHA. She said, "We started home schooling at the beginning of the second grade because our son was unable to handle the classroom environment. We home schooled Matthew alone for one year and then all three children for three or four years after which the older two went back to a small church school. Our son remains home schooled and seems to do well one-on-one."

Su of Wisconsin told of Ben, now 20 years old, who came home one day from 7th grade in public school and announced, "I'm going to get through high school and I'm not going to know a donkey from a peanut." Ben was EMR-Educable Mentally Retarded which was severe in his younger years. Su knew of no other parents educating special-needs children but one lady did encourage her to emphasize his *strong points*. She was able to teach Ben to read very well. Ben now has his drivers license, has a full time job and just moved into his own apartment, 35 miles from home. Su said, "Our God is a God of promises and hope!"

Fay, of South Carolina, said about schooling her Heather, who has Downs,

> *Home school for Heather was never a question. We had home schooled our other 5 children since 1979. All of them graduated from home school. Therefore Heather fell into her other siblings' tracks, although when my husband pastored a church in New York state, we put her into the public school system for one year. They put her into a class of mentally disabled children (about 12) in a classroom within an elementary school. She rode the bus from 5:30 a.m. each day and didn't arrive home until 5 p.m. Her days were very long and she was ill a lot of the time because of the exposure to all kinds of things in this school. Her learning was on a limited basis and in fact the whole experience was a waste of her time and health. All-in-all, it was a bad experience.*

Ginia of Maryland said,

> *I chose to home school mainly because after he was in school 3 years, the specialized program required Andrew (with Downs) to go all day to school. I felt he was too young. I decided to home school my daughter because in sending her to pre-school for a year, she cried all year and I figured out she learns better one-on-one. Andrew <u>loves</u> to be at home. It just felt like the right thing to do for both our children.*

Rosalie of Kansas said, "We were in our 10th year of home education when Harmony was born with Downs, she is now only 3fi and we are planning to educate her at home."

Does Home Schooling Require That Parents Have a Teaching Degree?

I know if we had considered educating Nathan at home full time, we probably would have felt we were not qualified. Why do we parents think we need an educational degree to teach our children? Since we had to tutor Nathan so that he could make it through public school, I worked with him on English and literature while Ellis did the math and science. History would have been so much easier with one of the home education history books which include our Christian heritage. History is a subject our whole family loves so we were always reading books outside the text book with Nathan.

Verna, of Kansas, home schooling her five, has a college degree in elementary education and a masters in guidance and counseling. She said, "Neither degree helped; they hindered my teaching using Biblical principles."

Fay from North Carolina who home schooled her five including the youngest, Heather, who has Downs, said, "I graduated from high school and have a diploma from a 'commercial course.' This was basically a high school course majoring in typing, book keeping and the so-called secretarial course. Since then I have gone on to get my Bachelor of Science Degree in Business management."

Mary Ann of Kansas, who home schooled the youngest of her six from the 7th grade, said, "I do not have a college degree. I had day care in my home and taught Sunday school and vacation Bible school for years."

Selena from Kansas said, "I have one year of business education." She now teaches all her children at home.

Janie of Oregon wrote, "I have four years of liberal arts college but due to a switch in majors, I didn't graduate. I am liberal arts educated half teacher and half nurse."

Kathy of Texas said, "I have a bachelor of fine arts in painting and drawing, a 12-hour minor in French, 9 hours of graduate education, 10 years of Down's Syndrome and home schooling. I have earned a degree in education haven't I? I've read every book in print on D.S. and all of the major books for home schooling. The answer is 'no'—I have no degree in education."

Sheila of North Carolina said, "I don't believe you need a college degree to be able to teach your children. It comes naturally."

Valerie of Massachusetts wrote, "My husband and I have no college degrees or degrees of any kind. However we know our children."

Janice of Kansas said, "I don't have a degree, however my college studies were in early childhood education. You would think that would be a great background, however it didn't include any special education courses. So most of what I learned didn't prove beneficial for working with my children."

Marilyn of Pennsylvania wrote, "I was a teacher for nine years before Timothy was born. Many leaders I admired were advocates of home schooling with a commitment to raise up Godly children with Godly values. My husband and I felt home schooling would be best. We've always home schooled Timothy, 15, Jonathan, 13, and now Steve, 15, who just came to live with our family."

Although some of the mothers whom I interviewed did have college degrees, most didn't feel that an educational degree significantly helped in teaching their children or was necessary.

Are Parents Encouraged to Home Educate Children with Special Needs?

In the early 1980s our neighbors and friends from church chose to home educate their children. At that time, Ellis and I questioned the wisdom of that decision. It didn't take long for us to learn, as we became better informed, that they had made a very wise choice. But even now, years later, parents who choose to home educate are still considered a little odd. If they choose to keep their special-needs child home for education they may be told they are missing out on the advantages offered by the public school. School authorities and Social Rehabilitation Services may accuse them of abusing their child. Regardless of the problems, Nathan could have better handled his schooling if we had taught him at home.

Sharon, of British Columbia, said about home schooling their adopted sons with Downs,

> *We never received any encouragement to teach our special-needs kids at home, in fact it has been just the opposite! Other than my home schooling friends and those that I corresponded with, most people think we are absolutely crazy.*

Fay, mother of an 11 year old with Downs in South Carolina said,

> *I did not know of anyone who was teaching a special-needs child at home. I received no encouragement to teach Heather at home. In fact, all school authorities thought that it would be best that she get a "public school education." I still do not know anyone who teaches their child at home. I wish I did, it sure would be a help to us locally.*

Janice of Kansas said,

> *We really didn't know anyone home schooling special-needs children*

when we started. My brother-in-law did home school their children and suggested that we contact Dr. Raymond Moore's organization. We contacted them and they encouraged us to try home schooling; we used their curriculum the first year. There was another family in our community with a son with Down's Syndrome; however, that family decided to send their child to public school.

Sheila of North Carolina was told by their neurologist about Katye (8 years old) who has epilepsy and is behind in developmental skills, "never, under any circumstance put her in public schools." Sheila continued, "He said that the best place for her was at home. We were floored, a professional *for* home schooling. We home school all our children. They have never been in any other school setting. We have never been ones to follow the crowd. We were unaware of any other special-needs children who were home schooled. We were on our own when it came down to it. My family was not *keen* on the idea for any of our children."

Sandy of New York, told of the problems their adopted Sarah, 16 years old, had in the public school. Sarah is blind and profoundly retarded and had severe eating problems. One day Sandy dropped by the public school unannounced and found the teacher holding Sarah from behind her wheelchair and force feeding her. Sandy said, "No wonder we had eating problems. We were told that we couldn't home school Sarah because of her many handicaps. We were gullible for a while but others told us differently and we suddenly became overwhelmed with information on home schooling. It took us too long to realize God's commands on teaching also applied to Sarah. We pulled her out of public school when she was 10 and she has been home educated since."

Kathy of Texas had never thought of home schooling until she gave birth to their second daughter with Down's Syndrome and met a neighbor who was home schooling her two older boys.

> *I asked many questions and I knew in my heart that home schooling would be best for the girls; Robin, our first born and Sarah, the little angel with DS, she softened my heart and slowed me down long enough to realize I had been pushing Robin toward being a burned out superbaby.*
>
> *The question is: is home schooling right for our children? Is it working? Is Sarah doing the most she is capable? Is Robin receiving enough "social" learning? YES! That means both girls have participated in various activities; choir, softball, track team, skating each week, field trips,*

Sunday school, AWANA. *Yet more importantly, they both are learning at their own pace, in their own way, with appropriate materials, with acceptable content, without pressure to complete work that might be meaningless anyway (you know, pegs in the pegboard stuff).*

Linda of Minnesota, whose adopted son has Klinefelters Syndrome which affects him physically in several ways like severe expressive speech delay, told us,

> *The decision to home school our child with special needs was an obvious one, as we had already been home educators of our three girls for four years at the time of his placement. We had joined ATII (Advanced Training Institute International), which encourages total family participation although they also encouraged us to seek outside expertise and therapy as needed.*

The decision on where your special-needs child will be educated must be thought through very carefully. Even when our Nathan was in public school in the '70s and '80s, we could not leave the decisions up to the educational experts. We had to be involved in every area. If a parent doesn't want their child labeled (which will probably be his lot for the rest of his school life) and would rather be told than asked how to best teach your child, be very cautious about placing your child in public school. The ridicule by his peers along with the labeling by the educational psychologists left Nathan with unhappy memories all his life.

Labeling by either the doctors or professional educators can be detrimental to your child. Sometimes the child uses his label as an excuse to not behave or do his work. But how others use it can be far worse. Phyllis Schlafly of Eagle Forum said, "Hanging derogatory labels on children has become big business in the public schools. The public schools get much more money if the child is labeled as having some defect."[2]

Dr. Thomas Sowell who has written the excellent book, *Inside American Education*[3] wrote an article in the August 1, 1994 *Forbes Magazine*,[4] page 55, about his son and other children who are slow maturing. His complete article was very helpful, and one area that he mentioned in particular was about the preschool testing that is done for three and four year olds. He said that the testing for hours by strangers in a strange setting can get any child upset, yet the results of that testing can result in lifelong decisions for that child.

Tom Hunsberger, who has taught special education in Maryland public schools for twenty years, told me that it was humanly impossible for him to meet the educational needs of the forty child caseload that he has. This is what I hear over and over again from good teachers who work in special education. They do not have the time or staff to meet the varied needs of the special-needs children.

Why Home Educate Your Child with Special Needs?

Here are the reasons I feel that home education is absolutely the best option for special-needs children (and all children).

1. Parents know their children better than anyone.

2. Parents can teach Biblical principles daily and implement them into the learning process. Proverbs 6:20-22

3. Parents can build a close relationship with their children so that they respect parental authority. Ellis could see that when he was in school fifty years ago, they were encouraging the children to question their parents' authority.

4. The only way a parent is going to know what their child is taught, is to do the teaching.

5. With home education you can adapt the amount and speed to the needs and health of your child.

6. Home education allows time to teach life skills along with academics. There is time for apprenticeships etc.

7. GOD ADMONISHES PARENTS TO TEACH THEIR CHILDREN.

God has given parents the wisdom, knowledge and responsibility to educate our children. No one else will care for or understand our child as well as we, the parents, even if we don't have a degree in education. There is a wealth of home school education materials based on Biblical principles and there are home school support groups to encourage and inform parents.

NOTES:

[1] Home School Legal Defense Association, P.O. Box 159, Peaonia Springs, Virginia 22129. Phone 703-388-2733.

[2] *Phyllis Schlafly Report* 1994. You may subscribe to her monthly letter for $20 a year from: Eagle Forum Trust Fund, Box 618, Alton, Illinois 62202.

This is excellent material from a Christian lawyer and teacher.

3 *Inside American Education* by Thomas Sowell 1993. The Free Press A Division of Macmillan, Inc. 866 Third Ave., New York, New York 10022.

4 "Autistic...or just shy?" Dr. Thomas Sowell, *Forbes*, August 1, 1994 page 55 (used by permission from Dr. Sowell)

CHAPTER SEVEN
Special Abilities! My Child?

1 Corinthians 12:4
"Now there are diversities of gifts, but the same Spirit."

Those Special Abilities May Turn Up Early

As a special-needs child matures, it is not unusual to ask or think, "What can this child do in life?" Especially when the physical and mental problems are more profound so that they are kept from what the world calls success. I am sure many parents grieve knowing that their child, because of the mental and physical limitations, is kept from accomplishing what we, as parents, think is important. Maybe that causes us to miss the special abilities that God has given them.

I don't remember complaining to God specifically about Nathan's lack of accomplishment but that may have been because the daily pressure to get Nathan through his studies and trying to keep him from eating all the time, kept me from thinking about the "what ifs." We did notice some unusual abilities in Nathan quite early. One was his ability to remember names of anyone he had met. Since my memory for names is horrible, I depended on him to rescue me from embarrassment. This ability helped his relationship with all he met.

Another gift we noticed in Nathan was an unusual ability with animals. He could tame new kittens that no one else could catch. He had the patience that animals trusted. He would sit by the hour waiting to pet a wild kitten and before long would be carrying him around the farm. Cats were his friends. He usually had a dozen or so that he meticulously fed each with their own dish. He would stay beside them until they were fed to make sure that one didn't take more than his share. His huge fat cats followed him everywhere.

Pets are excellent for special-needs children to take the pressure off the parents to meet all their child's emotional needs. Many times they can relate to an animal friend easier than they can with people. Nathan's pets were his friends and listeners to his troubles. He usually had one of the farm cats trained to stay in his room for a few hours each day. When he had a rough day, he would disappear to "talk" to his cats.

Nathan would pamper a sick cat, duck, goat or dog with more empathy than most people receive. He would carry a crippled duck for hours to protect it from his well-fed cats. When his baby goat strangled on its rope, Nathan handled it much better than I did. He buried it with all due respect while I shed tears in the house for Nathan's hurt. It could be that Nathan's love for animals was his start in his love and concern for hurting people. He was the first to remind our family to pray when he heard about someone who was sick or hurting. His concern for handicapped people never ceased to amaze me. Our small local hospital provided care for head-injury patients. Nathan started visiting them on a regular basis. Even though their speech was garbled from their injury, Nathan would spend hours visiting with different ones. He knew what they were saying because he took the time to listen. *I wondered if Nathan would have a job working with those whom others had no time to listen to and encourage.*

The hospital administrator saw that Nathan related well with these patients so she asked if he could teach a Bible study to five or six residents each week. Nathan's Bible story records were put to use again. He would choose a story and put it on tape. With my help he would write out questions to ask the patients. He did well for several weeks, but the patients would argue with each other or him which frustrated him. He didn't know how to handle it and the hospital wasn't always able to provide a nurses' aid to help him. He finally had to go back to sharing God's Word one-on-one. Sometimes he would sing or pray with those who could not speak.

A friend told me that when Nathan was in his twenties he had followed her outside after a Bible study class and gave her a hug and cried with her because her sister was so ill with cancer. He was so sensitive to the needs of others. He did the same thing for the family, and especially for me when he saw that I was discouraged or sick. For two weeks he took care of me when I was flat in bed with the flu following the wedding of our daughter and later when I had major surgery.

Nathan loved his abundant supply of books that he had purchased but if he thought one of them might help someone, he would loan it with the reminder that he wanted it back. His books were his friends.

Sandy from New York tells of their fifteen year old adopted Sarah who is totally blind and has cerebral palsy.

She has the unusual ability to love and show that love. She is like a puppy, so forgiving of everyone instantly and ready to give a hug. She learned to count by giving kisses on the cheek. If you ask for 3 or 7 or 14 kisses that's what you get. We count along with her, but she always stops at the right number. Her loving has been what has attracted so many people to her ministry. She has a beautiful smile and is an extremely happy child. She says, "Hi" and immediately reaches her arms up for hug. She constantly gives us the opening to tell someone about the Lord. She's our biggest blessing and God's love just shines through her.

Sarah was adopted as a baby when they had five other children ranging in ages of ten to sixteen.

Laura, from Michigan, whose seven year old son, Gideon has Williams Syndrome told that he has exhibited musical talent. Being the middle child of five children, he has already shown a gift for playing by ear. They love to sing together.

Parents Hold the Key to Unlocking Those Special Abilities

It may not be obvious right away what special talent or gift your special-needs child may have but that talent is only released through the perseverance of the parent.

May Lemke, in the book *May's Boy*[1] is an example of a parent who persevered when there seemed no hope. Leslie was six months old when May was asked if she would care for this little baby who was severely handicapped and was not expected to live. His eyes had been removed because they had become swollen, he had cerebral palsy and was retarded and his parents didn't want him. May's work as a nurse-governess had earned her a reputation around Milwaukee for being excellent with children. She agreed to take little Leslie even though it had been years since she had raised their own five children.

She fed and cared for him, but she was at a loss to help him physically. He remained silent and helpless year after year. May prayed that God would show her what to do. She talked to him constantly, took him everywhere with her. Although tiny herself, she carried him into the stores for her shopping. Finally at nine years of age, she and her husband, Joe, tried taking Leslie into the lake near their home. After several weeks with no response from Leslie either physically or verbally, he began to move his hands. May was so excited.

May walked with him strapped to her waist day after day. People told her that she was wasting her time but she said, "I believe God and He is going to do it. If God says He can do things, then He can do them for me.

If He doesn't, then I'm going to pester Him to death." Slowly Leslie learned to walk holding on to a fence. Physical therapists said they couldn't promise anything that would help him so May continued on her own.

When Leslie was twelve years old, May began to pray a new prayer for her son. She prayed that he might have a gift, something to give his life meaning. Several times a day, she implored, "Dear Lord, the Bible says that you gave each of us a talent. Please help me find the talent in this poor boy who lies there most of the day and does nothing." May bought Leslie a piano when he was thirteen years old. It seemed silly but May could play a little by ear. She had it put in Leslie's bedroom which almost filled up the room.

She played a few tunes for him and said "You see, love, that's music. That's part of God's language." Leslie loved music and would sit listening to records or the radio for hours, head down, serious, intense, a study of concentration.

Then, in his sixteenth year, something May calls "The Miracle" occurred.

At 3 a.m. May awoke and thought she heard music. She checked the television but it was off. She heard Tchaikovsky's Piano Concerto No. 1 coming from Leslie's room. She opened the door to find him playing like a professional, racing up and down the keys, never missing a note, as if he had been practicing for years.

May fell to her knees and cried. She ran for her husband. They both were on their knees for most of the night praising God and thanking Him for giving their boy the gift of music.

Leslie couldn't walk alone and had never gotten out of bed by himself before, yet somehow he had slid out of his bed and pulled himself up on the piano bench and begun to play. May called every one of their friends and Leslie's doctor to tell them about his talent. Leslie played for anyone who came. Any song that he had ever heard, he could play. His body began to fill out and he grew taller after he was seventeen. His hands, his body and all his senses seemed to be coming alive.

Leslie continued to play and sing for visitors who came to the Lemke home as well as performances at nursing homes, hospital and churches— before his first formal concert in 1974. He played for the Waukesha County Fair and drew the largest crowd ever assembled at the county exposition grounds.

Every time Leslie gave a concert, he could play anything they called out to him to play from hymns to classical. He could sing impersonations of well known singers. The audiences wanted his performances to continue for hours, but May would finally call it to a close.

If May had quit as others told her to do, Leslie would have never done

Special Abilities! My Child?

anything. He probably would not have lived. Through the help and wisdom God gave her and Joe, they prepared him for the special gift that God gave. Not every special-needs child will have a miraculous gift but they can find the place that God has for them in life.

Ellen in Kansas said that her Becky, who has Down's Syndrome, loves people and earnestly prays for them. She has a remarkable memory for songs, people's names and faces (even after not seeing them for years.) Ellen says, "I sing Christian songs to her almost every day to keep up her repertoire. She also knows simple foreign language songs. (Ellen, her mother knows several languages.)

Fay in South Carolina said that Heather, who has Downs, is called the "greeter" by the church people. She shakes hands with everyone and is very friendly, almost too friendly. "We've had to caution her about this. As far as abilities go she has about the same abilities of our other children but is much slower doing them."

Ben, age 19, of Wisconsin had severe EMR (educable mentally retarded) problems in his younger years. His mother Su said, "He has a real gift of relating to people. He holds two jobs. One is in a nursing home where he is EXCELLENT with the residents." Su home educated Ben from the seventh grade.

Selena in Kansas, says of Stephanie, 14, the oldest of her three girls, "She is very neat and orderly, she likes things in their place at all times and is very good with young children. If I can't find something, I just ask Stephanie and she can find it."

Sheila, of North Carolina, told of seven year old daughter, Katye who has epilepsy which causes her to process things differently in her brain. "She is very gifted artistically, but she only draws in black and white, she can't understand colors yet. We did arrange for art lessons which she has taken but her teachers said she had never seen such a young talented child and really didn't know how to teach her. She draws amazing pencil sketches." Jackie of Colorado tells of her eight year old son, "Christopher can name and use tools as well as the ability to tear down and rebuild different engine parts. He is enrolled in Taekwondo and has shown great ability to concentrate."

Linda of Minnesota said that their eight year old adopted son, who has Klinefelter's Syndrome, can lead them to numerous McDonald's restaurants, parks and branch libraries inspite of his severe physical problems. "In fact he remembers events that occur at places we visit only once and recalls and tells them to us frequently when we pass those places." She has not had a great deal of success with teaching reading even though she is home educating him as she has done with their three daughters.

Cindy of Kansas with seven year old Randon, who has Prader-Willi syndrome, said, "He is very musically inclined or anything that has to do with acting or being the center of attention. He gets up and pretends he is the preacher and has a whole sermon." She doesn't feel he is ready for music lessons yet.

Karen in Kansas said, "Christine in kindergarten can do her sister's second grade spelling, asks profound questions and has complex problem solving abilities. Having a gifted visually impaired child poses some interesting problems. She is still far behind in large motor skills."

Marilyn in Pennsylvania said of Timothy, "Because of the lack of use in his left arm, the right arm has become very strong. Thus he's a great basketball free-throw player. He just won first place at the McDonald's contest in the 14-17 year category."

Jane from Oregon told of Philip, "He could actually be classified as Savant (special ability) in his word comprehension. His ability to remember details from stories and chapel illustrations fascinated his teachers long before we discovered that he was autistic. His sculpting abilities are really God's gift to him as our state is horrible in its ability to provide employment for its handicapped. Most disabled spend a ridiculous amount of time in self entertainment as in southern Oregon. Philip has a small business in creating and selling small sculptures. His dogs are amazing considering he is self taught.

Ginia wrote from Maryland about Andrew, "He is incredibly creative. He made *any* item around the house into a toy and will entertain himself for very long periods of time. He is able to watch a TV show or video (Barney—he loves) and after seeing it two times he knows every gesture in the movie. He *loves* music. He likes to sing and listen to music and dance.

Marsha of Missouri told of Jessica, age thirteen, "She is very intuitive and has a deep understanding of psychological and abstract concepts as well as interpersonal relations. She's very analytical, emotionally mature and spiritually discerning. She has an extensive vocabulary, well-developed sense of humor, and displays musical ability through playing the piano.

Travis, the 16 year old son of Debbie of Kansas is very creative and imaginative. He loves to work with his hands using legos, is making detailed drawings of electrical or technical things. She said, "He still has a difficult time concentrating on most subjects, but give him the computer or legos and he will work for six to eight hours at a time. He has selective concentration at a high degree."

Evelyn of Kansas said of Kari, her 24 year old daughter, "I feel that Kari will make it on her own. She is a good worker and very dependable. She is becoming more independent. She reads her Bible daily. I believe that God will help her be very successful in her job."

Sarah of Texas with Downs is age eleven. Kathy, her mother said, "Sarah loves to pray, talk about Bible characters and stories and sing. I believe her ability to read is unusual as well as her speech which is understandable."

Mary of Indiana told of their son, Gary, who is twenty one. She said, "He is very good at drawing and woodworking. He loves to build things out of wood."

As I read over the interviews with parents, I saw a common thread, music often stimulated and encouraged development in special-needs children. Also special-needs children can be gifted in relationships with others. Whatever their talent may be, they seem to be able to excel in one special area.

Parents can and should provide the equipment, lessons, and encouragement for their special needs child to develop that area God has gifted them. It will take longer to learn but once they accomplish the lessons, they are a blessing to themselves and others. The achievement in a certain area does wonders to give the special-needs child confidence and a useful purpose in life.

NOTES:

[1] Shirlee Monty, *May's Boy* (Thomas Nelson Publishers, Nashville, 1981), 100-104

CHAPTER EIGHT
How Does a Special-Needs Child Respond Spiritually?

> *1 Samuel 16:7*
> *"...For man looks at the outward appearance, but the Lord looks at the heart."*

Love for God Is Not Limited by Mental Ability

Early in Nathan's life he displayed an avid interest in learning about God and the Bible. Being our youngest, I think we just expected him to join in whatever we were doing with the older children. Since his special gift was listening and remembering what he heard, Bible stories were never forgotten and he wanted more. He remembered what we read in the Bible better than his brother and sister, who were four and six years older. He never tired of hearing those 40 Bible story records. Repetition is necessary for all children, but especially so for those with limited mental ability.

Nathan, seven at the time, was eating breakfast one morning. Out of the blue he said, "Daddy, do you hope I go to heaven?" Taken by surprise, Daddy answered, "Huh?"

Nathan then answered his own question with, "You have to be sorry for your sins and ask Jesus to be your Savior don't you. I did that didn't I?" He had said at age five that he wanted to go to heaven to be with Jesus and wanted to pray about it at supper one evening.

Nathan was talking to me at this age about heaven and who would go there. He said, "Julie, a four year old, won't go she's bad." I don't know why he thought she was bad. Children his age often made hurtful remarks to him, especially at school.

He loved to take my flannel graph Bible stories for Sunday school and tell them at age six and seven. He did unusually well considering that he couldn't read at that time. He even had voice changes for the different characters and asked questions afterwards. I had gone over the story with him earlier. *I could see that Nathan worked well telling Bible stories to young children. That might be the job that God had for him.*

Janice from Kansas said of her son, Lucas, with Down's Syndrome,

> *These children may be physically and mentally handicapped but they are not spiritually disabled. God can quicken the spirit of any child and that spirit can grow. He focuses on the heart not the mentality. Both Lucas and Jennifer with Cerebral Palsy memorize Bible verses. It is a struggle and it takes longer for them to learn than other children. We've bought them tapes and they have learned lots of verses and hymns by listening and singing along. Bible is a major course and we use stories to practice reading, as reference to character studies, and as a part of history.*

Fay from N. Carolina told of Heather (12 years), the youngest of her six children,

> *Heather has heard since her birth (with Downs) all about Jesus and God. Because her dad is a minister, she has always been involved with church situations. Her school work has things in it now and then about Jesus. She prays before her meals and at bedtime and at any other time when she wants to ask God for help or has a request for someone else. She has prayed the prayer of salvation to accept Jesus as her Savior, after repeating the words I said. If she understands all this only God knows, we do not know for sure.*

Debbie of Kansas said of Travis, who was labeled by the public school as autistic, "Travis has had several special testimonies in his short lifetime. He has been a great asset to our daily devotions at 7:00 a.m. We pray over our children. My husband is truly the spiritual head of the family and takes the headship of his children seriously."

Leadership of the Family is the Husband's Responsibility — God's Principle

Once I understood that God gave the husband the heavy responsibility for leading the family both spiritually and physically, it was a load off my training the children. I had tried pushing my husband to have formal everyday family devotions. We tried it for awhile but it didn't work well with Nathan because his attention span and understanding were so far behind the other two. Instead my husband chose to use teachable moments with the children when he took them with him in the car or pickup or the times they climbed in bed with him for story time.

A mother can do much to encourage a husband to take leadership of the family. This builds a stability that gives security to all children especially to those with learning problems. If there is no father in the home, a child needs a mature man to model. Those who know more than I do say that a child receives his concept of God from his father. A grandfather, an uncle or mature Christian from church could fill that important role. God says that He is Father to the fatherless and husband to the widow, so God will provide as we seek His plan.

I thought that we, as a family, should memorize scripture every day and pushed for that. Ellis thought we should model for the children daily reading of the Bible either to them or alone. Rote memorization was not that important to him. He felt that as they became familiar with the Bible, it would almost become second nature to them. I didn't agree but as the spiritual leader he was the one accountable to God. Now that our two oldest are married, I can see that he was right. In their own families they build their decisions around Biblical principles. Our daughter has Bible verses displayed around the house as part of their home education.

There isn't anything wrong with scripture memory, in fact, later all our children joined a Scripture memory program to earn a trip to camp. Nathan did make it to camp but it was not enjoyable, the kids were cruel to him. One boy even squirted shaving cream on Nathan's face while he slept.

At the age of seven, Nathan hid his dirty clothes under his bed and I scolded him. He said "That's sin isn't it Mommy, I've got to ask Jesus to forgive me." So we prayed about it. He had trouble understanding math concepts but he understood what sin was.

Nathan had a depth of love and a special ability to discern when others were hurting. Our family is not a real hugging family but Nathan often came up to me when I was troubled and would give me a hug or say, "Let's talk to Jesus about this." As we parents nurture this special gift in our children, others will see Jesus in them.

Nathan felt accepted in our church. He worked with the pastor at different times on special projects. He went to Sunday school with the "normal" children. They didn't include him in their social events outside the church but at church he was accepted.

One morning following a difficult week with his health problems, Nathan and I were in our small town. He especially wanted to purchase Easter baskets for his niece and nephew, who were three and nine years old at that time. Stopping at the hospital at his insistence, Nathan went to visit

Kenny who couldn't talk because of his head injury. Nathan came out excitedly saying, "Kenny was awake today so I could talk to him." Kenny looked forward to Nathan's visits as did many of the head injury patients and the long-term care elderly. He had time for them. He wanted to share Christ with them.

Rosalie of Kansas said that Harmony, the youngest of her seven children, likes to "read" the Bible at age four. Harmony was born with Down's Syndrome. "We pray together, sing action songs and read Proverbs a chapter at a time. Proverbs has worked well as speech training also because she loves to repeat the last word of a phrase. We consider training in obedience as a vital part of her spiritual training ("If ye love Me, keep My commandments.") So we try to see that commands are carried out."

Rosalie continued "There is no one like 'Daddie.' Harmony climbs up on his lap in the evenings and they talk and count and play." A father teaches through so many ways while mothers have a different role which is the daily living lessons.

Valerie from Massachusetts, whose eight year old daughter, Megan, has Downs, finds that by home educating her daughter, she can pray before eating and talk about the Lord during the day—something she couldn't do if she was in public school. "We want to put more of *God* into her education. I'm not sure I'm seeing signs that she understands what I share spiritually, I think it is harder for her because it's not something as concrete as some of the academic lessons. But I will never give up though it may take a longer time. She will *learn spiritual lessons and that's my greatest joy.* Megan has told me when going into a dark room she won't be scared because Jesus is with us."

Laura from Michigan, whose son Gideon has Williams Syndrome, says that at age seven he attends church and quietly moves from family to family, sitting next to whoever will pet him awhile. He doesn't sit still well, so he doesn't do too well in Sunday school. He just lives God's love for people. "We haven't 'worked' with him really on anything-spiritual or academic. We just live out our daily lives, dependent on God. We pray together every night. He prays for the sick. He asked Jesus into his heart a few months ago. I don't know if he truly understands…maybe he knows better than I."

Provide Materials That Will Make Spiritual Training Easy for Your Child with Special Needs.

Terry and Robert of Maryland, whose adopted son, Stephan, (age 10) has Downs, use Moody Bible Institute's videos, and provide Bible story tapes. "We believe that since God is a spiritual being He speaks to our spirits and that Stephan's spirit should be filled with God's Word even if his mind cannot yet grasp certain teaching. Because of this belief, we take him with us into church instead of sending him to children's church. He has learned to be able to sit through the whole service and amazes us, at times, with how much he is retaining."

Cindy, of Kansas, said of her Prader-Willi eight year old son, "It has been most interesting because he is so open to receive what we teach him about God. He loves Sunday school and church and the music. He prays every night. His little 2 year old cousin died and Randon talks about her being with Jesus; that she is in heaven. His understanding of that is way beyond that which I thought possible. He is so trusting and eagerly accepts all we teach while his older brother is more questioning. He seems to understand Jesus living in his heart."

Sarah, the 16 year old adopted daughter of Sandy, of New York, has been in church from day one. Sandy said, "she has always had a sense of quietness when others are quiet. When ANYONE prays, she is silent and as soon as AMEN is out, her mouth runs. She says only about 12 words or significant sounds, but she says them thousands of times a day. Because her IQ has been established in the 10-20 range, we don't know how much understanding she has spiritually, but she listens to gospel music all the time. If she is somewhere rock music is playing, she gets visibly unhappy about it. Her tapes are a testimony and witness to the public health nurses who come in on a regular basis to assist in showers and respite. She has given us an open door to witness and lead several women to Christ."

Kathy of Texas, told of Sarah, her ten year old with Downs, "She is a believer. When she was seven, she said that she desired to be a child of God—she wanted Jesus. We prayed and she sang, *Jesus is my Lord, my Master, my Savior.* Some mornings she comes down the stairs singing to the Lord or pretends to be a Bible character. She listens to much scripture music, knows many Bible characters and stories (her memory is excellent). She can recite many scriptures and spontaneously sings praise songs. She can read her Bible and mine (NKJ) as well."

From Minnesota Linda and Phil told of their adopted son, the youngest of their four children. He has Klinefelter's Syndrome. At nine years of age he worships with their family and even urges others to do so. He requests prayer from their pastor but does not sit still or quietly during church.

Jackie from Colorado told of Christopher, her eight year old who has Golden-Hars Syndrome. He is slow mentally but *not delayed.* Jackie said, My children all seem to have a basic understanding of God. Always my biggest question to them is, 'Is that what Jesus would do?' *Spirituality is a lifestyle—not a Sunday thing."*

From North Carolina, Sheila wrote about two of her four children. She said, "Their spiritual development has not been hindered by their problems. We use KONOS which is a Bible-based character traits curriculum. We give God the glory and honor for creation and teach our children accordingly."

Could it be that children with special needs are given a special gift of love from God? Becky, a 25 year old from Wichita with Downs is so loving. She hugs everyone she meets and tells them she loves them. I ate lunch with her and Ellen, her mother. I received many hugs and was told, "You are beautiful" or "I love you," often during the meal.

As Janice of Kansas said,

> These children may be mentally or physically disabled but not spiritually handicapped." Nowhere in scripture are we told that God asks about a person's intelligence before allowing them to believe in Him and become His child. I Corinthians 1:20 and 27 says "Where is the wise? Where is the disputer of this age? Hath not God made foolish the wisdom of this world? God has chosen the foolish things of the world to confound the wise; and God has chosen the weak things of the world to confound the things which are might.

Mary of Indiana said of Gary, 21 years, "He tells others that God has given him an uncommon blessing when they ask him about his disabilities." Marsha and Terry in Missouri told of Jessica's spiritual understanding,

> When she was 2½, she asked us about accepting Christ as her Savior. We knew others would not accept a spiritual decision of that magnitude from one that young so we explained that to her and suggested that she wait until the time was right. She understood and agreed. The next Sunday she asked the pastor to carry her into his office to talk which he immediately did. She told him that she wanted to accept Christ as her Savior and explained the way of salvation to him. He knew that she understood and prayed with her.

Marilyn of Pennsylvania said that Timothy accepted the Lord when he was 8 years old. He has a heart for right and wrong and obedience. When he disobeys, he asks for forgiveness. Timothy at fifteen is a dependable worker, faithful and responsible who wants to honor God in his work.

Janie of Oregon wrote of her three autistic children,

> I have been awed to see how the Holy Spirit works to reveal Christ

to special-needs kids in unique ways tailored to each individual. In Jeremiah 29:13 it says that "*if you seek Me with your whole heart, you will surely find Me.*" When a handicapped child does this, Christ reveals Himself to each one uniquely, communicating truths which I am at a loss to explain. Each of our children with special needs have received Christ as Savior before the age of six and has had a perfect understanding and peace about it.

Karen of Kansas said, "Christine's grasp of spiritual concepts sometimes astounds us. She is growing like any normal child in this area. I suppose the day will come when she will have to deal with—'why did God make my eyes bad?'"

Ginia of Maryland told that Andrew with Down's Syndrome, reaches for their hands to pray and he is quiet in church. She said, "I always tell him that Jesus loves him."

Children with special needs can come to know God personally on their own level. They should be taught about Christ and trained to obey His principles just as normal children should. In a family it works best if the father is the spiritual leader as God has designed, but God will provide if that is not possible. We parents understand what works in teaching our child about God. We can't depend on someone else to do it for us.

Look for a church that will encourage you in your plans to apply Biblical principles for raising your special-needs child. Some of your best support teams are your Christian friends who will pray for and with you. Ask for their prayer support. Most won't know your specific needs unless you tell them. Many people in our small church were not aware of the struggles we were going through with Nathan. There were a few who were involved in helping us who knew the difficult situations we faced especially as his health deteriorated.

CHAPTER NINE
Socialization—Facts and Fiction

> *Colossians 3:16*
> *"Let the word of Christ dwell in you in all wisdom, teaching and admonishing one another in psalms and hymns and spiritual songs, singing with grace in your hearts to the Lord."*

Children With Special Needs Are Often Not Accepted by Normal Children

Socialization seems to come to the forefront of any discussion on whether children should be home educated. It is especially a problem for the child with special needs. And if they are home educated kids, the experts are sure they lack the right socialization. Parents of children with special needs have learned many lessons guiding their children through learning social skills.

Tyler, age nine and autistic, sometimes asks, "Why doesn't someone like me?" Jean, his mother said "I've always been people oriented and concerned about people and I struggle with Tyler's problem. I wasn't even supposed to have children. We had gone through testing to get pregnant. When I meet God, I want to ask, 'Why did You make people like this?' I'm sure all parents struggle with this."

It hurts a parent's heart to see children tease, ignore or treat unfairly their special-needs child. We can't force other children to include them in games or social events. How can we help our child through those difficult times?

Nathan didn't have any obvious evidence of his mental and physical problems yet at times children his own age would be terribly cruel. They would laugh when he fell asleep at school or on the bus. He couldn't stay awake even when he desired to do so. By the time he was in junior high, his extra weight also made him vulnerable to teasing. He lacked some of the understanding of social skills; mentally he couldn't comprehend them.

For most families who home educate, the closeness that parents have with the child gives the child a security to be able to handle the mistreatment they may find outside the home. Nathan had a good relationship with almost everyone in our small church. There were a few incidents of children near his age making life difficult for him but older children and adults were respectful to his inquisitive questions.

Junior high in the public school was very difficult for Nathan. He had one Christian friend who would bring him a tissue when he was crying from the hurtful comments. During his freshman year, in another building for the 9-12th grades, a senior boy from our church took Nathan under his wing those first few weeks of school. Being a popular boy, Brad let the other kids know that Nathan was his friend. Nathan cheered at all the home football and basketball games. The older kids gave him a special award for being such an enthusiastic sports fan. They had him sit with the cheering squad. He would play his baritone horn in the pep band and sit the rest of the evening right behind the cheerleaders. Even following Nathan's graduation from high school, members of that senior class were still friendlier than his own classmates.

The home is the best place to learn social skills without fear of rejection or laughter should the child make a mistake. Nathan could talk with anyone but at times while talking with girls, he couldn't discern when they were just being nice to him or wanted to date him. He didn't talk about it much but during the many stays in the hospital he was sure a young nurse wanted to date him. He didn't understand that she was just doing her job.

Parents that I interviewed talked of the difficult social situations their special-needs children encountered.

Sarah, of Texas, who is ten years old with Downs, finds that other children do not believe that she is ten. They stare, then shun her at field trips. Others are angry when she doesn't act her age. With familiarity and parental guidance, some children have accepted Sarah well. She has a small group of friends, two of the oldest are her age, the youngest is 7 years. Kathy, her mother said, "I *find that some public schooled children* have more TOLERANCE AND INTEREST in her, for who she is, what she has to say and her activities. Part of the reason for the distrust in the home schooling children could be because the children are tight-knit in their relationship. Then she enters the picture and 'threatens' their little group (normal response for children, I believe) HOWEVER, all her close girl friends are home schooled; their parents discuss Sarah's needs with their daughters, how to be friends etc. In terms of acceptance, these relationships are most firm."

Once a child is in public school with a label that requires them to have special teaching, the child automatically is treated as *different.* Inclusion (which is now used in some schools) rather than taking the child to a resource room, may help the child to some extent from being ostracized by the other children. For any child a small physical or mental problem will be noticed and become an object of talk by the other children. Parents and teachers can help to discourage this but can not stop it 100 percent. Recess, before and after school and riding the bus are the hardest for special-needs children. Much of the hurt Nathan suffered at school, he never shared with us. Maybe his sleeping the hour ride home on the bus was a blessing. During the time Nathan was in L.D. classes in the '70s, the children were taken from their regular classrooms for several hours each day. All the children who were in LEARNING DISABILITIES classes, were treated differently by the other children.

Dr. James Dobson said in *Preparing for Adolescence,* "Beauty, intelligence, and money are the three attributes valued most highly in our society."*1 If a child has none of these, he will never be included in the "in" circle. In our AWANA club, we have one third grade girl who was not able to read. Some of the other girls refuse to sit by her though she is cute and friendly. Maybe a child has to be all three to be accepted now.

Selena, from Kansas, said

> *Our Stephanie (15) goes everywhere we go and does everything that we do. We have an unbelievable amount of people with children in our home and she is with students through the home school group and church. She occasionally will have a friend from public school stay overnight. We don't make any special effort, she is just a part of the family. Special-needs children are sometimes without friends because they can't participate in normal events because their needs are more severe. Stephanie is more like a very shy child.*

From Massachusetts, Valerie said of Megan, her eight year old with Downs,

> *We feel it is unnecessary to make special efforts to find socialization situations for Megan. Contrary to what many people believe, school is not the only place children learn and utilize social skills. Children learn them from the family from infancy and continue to learn in all situations. Megan socializes at home, with neighborhood children and adults, at the store, visiting family and friends at church, at the doctor's office, at the bank, etc. In short, everywhere we go there is an opportunity to interact and socialize with all people of all ages and believe me, Megan certainly takes advantage of it.*

Sharon from British Columbia who has two adopted sons with Downs, and a twelve year old daughter labeled with ADD by the public school, said, "I don't go out of my way to find socialization for our children. I don't think that is important. Florena goes to Sunday school, Beavers, Girl Guides, gymnastics, etc. along with friends to play with."

Heather, the youngest of six children from South Carolina, who has Downs, lives far out in the country where her father is a pastor. Fay, her mother said,

> The only social situation she has is church and her older siblings. We do feel that it would be nice for Heather to have some friends with disabilities and we have tried to find a support group of some type. We did belong to a group of this type when we lived in Florida where she was born. We even tried to get her involved with special olympics but were told that we would need to work through her school to do this. Being home schooled, there was no possibility for this endeavor.

Nellie from Oklahoma said that her daughter, C.L. gets along with anyone.

> All ages of people are in the real world. It is only in the public school that you have to deal with people your own age. <u>Get Real</u>, we live with all ages, don't we? Socialization is no problem.

Christian Home Educators Association of California answered the question about socialization.

> This is perhaps the most misunderstood aspect of home education. Popular opinion holds that children need regular interaction with a large group of peers in order to acquire social skills. However, there is significant evidence that extensive peer contact causes peer dependency and low self-image. On the other hand, Godly principles of interaction can be reinforced when children play under supervision of Christian families which share common values. Freedom from peer pressure fosters self-confidence, independent thinking, the ability to relate to people of all ages, and improved family relations.[2]

What is the Real Need for Socialization?

According to Dr. Paul White, Ph.D. in psychology who specializes in working with children, said,

...social skills are those skills which people need in order to effectively relate to others. Numerous social skills have been identified: the skill of communicating one's thoughts, understanding others and replying to them, resolving conflicts, meeting and greeting others, understanding society's rules for behavior, being able to interpret other's body language and understanding a situation from another person's perspective.³

If that is what is required for socialization, where does that leave the child who can't talk clearly, can't hear, can't see, or doesn't understand body language? Does that mean that a child can't learn social skills? I don't think so—our children with special needs may be limited but with guidance and example they can learn what is acceptable.

From the interviews of parents, I see that families who are home educating find a closer relationship between the siblings. That isn't always true when the children are out of the home eight to ten hours a day. There isn't time to build close relationships. During the day while home educating, the other children can work with the special-needs child, learning as well as helping. What better way to teach the acceptance of all people regardless of their mental or physical ability?

Andrew in Maryland, who has Downs, goes on field trips and family swim and play times. Ginia, his mother said, "If anyone is 'afraid' of special-needs children or adults, they should spend a day with Andrew and they'd be cured. I adore Andrew. He has so much of God's love in his sweet smile."

Sheila of North Carolina told that Katye (7 years) and Huxley (5 years) are getting enough socialization without making a conscious effort to do so.

Mary Ann in Kansas whose son Tyler, has now graduated from home education high school, said "I didn't make any special efforts at socialization. Because he was slower in co-ordination, he avoided groups his age but swam a lot."

Kathy of Texas, who originally published the *NATHHAN* Magazine, wrote about Sarah who has Downs,

Ah, socialization! At first I was very conscious of the "social time" she had because I was writing IEPs (Individual Educational Plan) for her for Hewitt when she was three years or so. She went to Mother's Day out once a week, AWANA, Sunday School and field trips. We have dropped Mother's Day Out (She was too old at six though they allowed her one extra year at the kindergarten level) She has my husband's and my personality; we work well (best) alone or with one friend. Sarah prefers to play alone with her dolls or games. She gets exhausted when she is around too many children for too long. Because we live out in the country, and because Sarah prefers to be alone or with us and there are no neighbors near, she spends little time with friends her age. She spends a lot of time with older children at the theater or ball park with Robin, her older sister and her friends....I am even more convinced that "control" over social activities is essential. Friendships should be encouraged in the context of a loving church on a limited basis.

Children With Special Needs Must Be Taught Correct Social Relationships.

Linda of Minnesota shared this idea in regard to their adopted son. She added:

> We take him with us as much as possible. We give him opportunities to place his order at fast food restaurants. We encourage him to interact with people at church and with the parents of children he plays with at neighborhood parks.

Jackie of Colorado told that Christopher (8 years) is teased by some and ignored by others while some ask questions about his face development due to Golden Harr Syndrome. She said,

> I feel with absolute belief that Christopher has thrived being home schooled. If he was enrolled in public school, he most definitely would not. At home Christopher receives unconditional love. He is supported, he has developed self-confidence. While he is learning his most important basics of reading, writing and math, he is not worried about being teased or made fun of with me as his teacher. I know exactly where he is in his learning. What teacher has the time and love to do this with each student? I would be bold in saying, I believe none. Who could tolerate slobbering, grouchiness etc. except his own mother. We know best how to motivate them.

Evelyn, of Kansas, told about Kari one of her twins. Kari is slow mentally, possibly from being nutritionally starved before birth. She said, "When Kari was young, she had several friends but as she grew older (she is 24) her friends became fewer and fewer."

Evelyn, who trained to be a teacher of special education after her daughters were in school, said,

> *In our high school classes for special-needs problems, we find without exception that the teenagers who will not respect authority and are behavior problems do not have a dad or they have a step-father they do not respect. Those kids rule their moms and the school.*

God's plan for the family is with a mother and father. When one is missing it affects children in more ways than we fully understand. A child without a father has problems adjusting socially. They need that male authority to give them security. For single parents, the extended family or a church group could help fill that need.

What If Your Child With Special Needs Is Severely Handicapped?

Sandy, of New York, wrote that Sarah (adopted) who is blind and profoundly retarded and with cerebral palsy, at fifteen goes with them most everywhere so she has contact with other children in their ministry.

> *She loves being with children in Sunday school even though she doesn't do anything but sit in her chair and listen and laugh. At first children are intimidated by her wheel chair and her aggressive outstretched arms wanting hugs but soon they warm up and respond well to her hugs.*

It has been several years since children and adults with mental limitations were kept from any social contact with "normal" people. They were either put in special homes, institutions or kept in the back bedroom of the family home. We have come a long way since that time but parents are the ones God has given the responsibility to teach the children how to best fit into social interaction. They must learn this *early* in their lives. To have friends one must be friendly. (Proverbs 18:24) That applies to children with special-needs also.

Harmony with Down's Syndrome is the youngest of 5 children in Kansas. Her family sings together and four-year-old Harmony goes with the family and waves to the people in the audience as they perform their program. Rosalie, her mother, said, "When her oldest brother ran for a public office, Harmony wore a special campaign outfit and many times people would stop her in the store and talk to her about her brother and her outfit." Harmony doesn't lack for social involvement.

There is no way a child with special-needs can escape being treated differently by their peers but guidance by loving parents can help prevent many of the mistakes that special-needs children can make in socialization. This is best done in a family setting or church situation where others have been taught by the parents how best to work with your child.

Jean of Kansas told about Tyler, her son who is borderline autistic,

> It is always a good idea to inform people who are working with your child. The baseball coach, the swimming coach or whoever works with your child. Tell them how to work with your child. Also the teachers at church so they will not be alarmed when he does something unusual in class. Tell them early on what to expect with your child. This will save the child and you a lot of problems.

Mary of Indiana wrote that for socialization she formed a home school group for special-needs families.

Laura of Michigan said, "We do not make any effort to socialize any of our children. They see other kids at church and they have a large extended family. Socialization is over-rated."

Marsha of Missouri wrote about Jessica, "We have her out in public and in social situations regularly. She makes it a social event on her own. We used to orchestrate special opportunities for socialization, but they always backfired."

Timothy of Pennsylvania has many activities to attend. Marilyn, his mother, said, "The church has mainly met the social needs he has. My husband is a pastor for Children's ministries at a very large church and thus we have many activities, home school co-ops and many friends."

Jane of Oregon told that they had been involved with Special Olympics and a Sunday school class for mentally handicapped called Special Angels, but found that was too stimulating for either Philip or Jon. Jon especially needs to know what is going to happen, how it will happen and when. Unexpected changes cause him to get really upset and throw tantrums. The Lord allowed them to purchase a small ranch which is a perfect low stimuli environment for the boys. She said "Cherish, her 10 year old daughter, has been forced gently into interaction and social contacts at school and she has had the benefit of being taught appropriate social responses. Now she begs to become a Girl Scout or do 4-H where a few years ago these would have been frightening."

Karen of Kansas said that Christine, six years old, loves to be around people, has lots of friends, some enemies and will talk to anyone who will listen. "We do not make special efforts for socialization. (She embarrasses Mom and Dad to tears during Children's sermons because she is so verbal)."

God in His sovereignty planned for this child for a special purpose. It wasn't an accident. The acceptance of this by the parents gives love and security to the child.

Why couldn't Jean's idea of informing be done with the parents and friends of the child with special needs. Children are wonderfully accepting once they know the reason for a problem. Just like the children who accepted blind Sarah who wanted many hugs. Once the children understood they warmed up to her. In the Learning Disabilities classroom, Nathan treated one little boy with severe physical problems very unkindly. Once we explained what the physical problem was and why we wouldn't allow Nathan to treat the boy unkindly, Nathan accepted him and helped him.

Just because our child has mental and physical disabilities doesn't mean that he can't have friends or learn social manners but parents will have to be involved. We can't just shove little Johnny or Susie out the door and say "go make friends." Go with them, include them on family outings and *teach them how to interact with others of all ages.* This will prepare the child for a variety of social situations.

NOTES:

[1] *Preparing for Adolescence* by Dr. James Dobson, 1978 by Vision House Publishers, Santa Anna, CA 92705, Page 27.

[2] Christian Home Educators of California, P.O. Box 28644 Santa Ana, CA 92799, from a special brochure prepared to answer common questions relating to home education.

[3] *What About Their Peer Relationships* by Paul E. White, Ph.D., 1994 Published by Family Resources, 9130 Barron, Wichita, KS 67207, page 3.

CHAPTER TEN
Guilt or Satisfaction

by Ellis Adee

Proverbs 4:1
"Hear my children the instruction of your father..."

Note from Donna:

Ellis encouraged me to write Nathan's story. After I had written several chapters, he said, "I'd like to write a chapter." He is an excellent Bible student and teacher but putting thoughts down in writing is difficult for him. But his spiritual leadership in our marriage and family has built the foundation for what I write and share. What he shares in this chapter is vital for all parents especially those whose children are born with special needs.

God's Design for Sex

Society has led us to believe in a perfect family with perfect children, perfectly spaced and perfectly behaved without one minute of inconvenience. This attitude is the mistake that we parents make and it is central and basic. Often our attitude is more like a tomcat towards kittens rather than according to God's design. In Psalm 27 God calls children arrows and He says He will bless the man who has his quiver full. I think we have misunderstood God's plan for sex. How does this affect our attitude towards our child with special needs?

Where can we start? I think there are several issues that need to be faced:

1. Few people would marry if it was not for God's designed desire and need for sexual fulfillment.

2. God's design is for His children to have a long term (on going) fulfilling sex life except during health problems. Song of Solomon; Adam at creation; Ephesians 5 "Cherish" and I Corinthians 7:1-5.

3. It is also God's design during the moment of our great mutual pleasure to create a new life (which we call conception). God controls the womb.

4. At the moment of conception all the characteristics of that new life have been decided by our sovereign God; including whether or not that new life will be less than perfect.

Back to our problem: often this creation concept of the sex life is pushed aside. The focus is on merely pleasure or convenience. This may seem to work out okay for a while *unless* you have an "unplanned" child, and God help us, if that child is handicapped and we have forgotten or ignored the fact that God chose this child for us. The worst thing we can do is to resent or reject at one level or another, a child who is not convenient. A handicapped child is *not convenient.*

To summarize this concept: If you can't accept a child with special needs, don't have children; if you don't want children, don't have sex; if you don't want sex, why get married?

This is where we get into trouble which effects the way we treat our children especially the child with special needs. We want the process but we want to control the product (child). That is not our role or choice! *It is God's.* All the rest that I have to say depends on this principle.

Let me tell you, that if you resent or reject *any* child, they in their heart of hearts will know it. This is even more true of a handicapped child who experiences daily rejection in many different ways. This resentment or rejection of ours is a spiritual problem. We can't blame God, clumsy doctors or society. The resentment is our problem and no one else's. God gave this child to *us.*

How do we overcome this resentment? First we need to view this handicapped child as a gift from God.

We took care of our son reasonably well but too much of the time it was out of duty and not with the attitude of God described in Proverbs 8:32 "…I delight in the sons of men." This handicapped one, we must love him and not merely put up with him out of duty. Do we *delight* in him? God knows your attitude and the child with special needs will soon find out!

Let me illustrate it from our life with Nathan. He had a work sheet of 32 math problems of simple addition like 2+3 … in school. He had messed around with three or four of the 32 problems. Since we had 15 minutes before bus time, I suggested, "Let's do these problems. I'll write while you tell me the answers. Okay?"

We began, but he soon complained that Father made numbers wrong so he took over the writing chore. With very little help or motivation from me, he finished the entire page in the 15 minutes. I was stunned.

Pouncing on the opportunity, I complimented him on his work and wove into the praise, "You can do this just like any kid." (Building up his self esteem) I asked, "Where did you get the idea that you couldn't do these problems? Who told you that you were too dumb to answer these problems like other kids?"

I will never forget his quiet, perceptive answer: *"Just about everybody."* You may not *tell* your child with special needs that they can't cut the mustard in those words but being growled at in our impatience, endlessly tested, pulled out of the class at school, etc. will tell them. If you don't cherish and delight in the child that you and God created, they will know and won't even attempt what they can achieve. The whole incident with the math questions took less than 15 minutes. Don't we parents have 15 minutes for that special child? At certain times it can be very important.

Some basic testing may be necessary but we found much of the testing is designed to prepare them for more testing! Know your child and monitor the "professionals" very carefully. Don't let them test your child beyond what the child can handle. In Deuteronomy 6 God has given the parents that responsibility. We didn't know about home schooling when Nathan was in school but we virtually did just that. Most of what Nathan received at school were his assignments. He didn't do the work there because he kept falling asleep, a result of the Prader-Willi problem. The socialization that he found in school was mostly bad with the exception of a few outstanding Christian kids who intervened to help him. Without them, it would have been a total disaster.

Nathan couldn't compete in academics or athletics, however he loved to cheer for others. We should have shown him how to do it more gracefully to keep him from being embarrassed. Whatever your special-needs child loves to do, show him how to do it as gracefully as he can so he won't suffer needlessly from his mistakes and ineptness.

The same God who "delights in you" as a child of His also is going to hold you accountable for how you take care of your new creation.

Where Is Our Focus?

What are the things that cause us to fail as parents? I think one is our focus as fathers on finding fulfillment in the wrong areas. We men have a tendency in our culture to focus on financial success, influence, position, and all the politically correct things. Think for a moment, how is your career affecting your wife? Is she growing "better" or "bitter?" Are you cherishing her, supporting her in the care of the children or causing her by your attitude to feel that she is standing alone.

The average, "good" parents cope with and do okay raising "normal" kids and mature themselves from the process. But when God chooses to give these "average good" parents a handicapped child, He plans to make that parent into a superb person. Would you rather find satisfaction in the kids you are entrusted with or pride yourself in the knowledge that you have a reputation as a financially successful and highly respected man? Wouldn't you have a more significant and lasting reward, though few may notice, to have children who are an improvement over yourself?

What about the perpetually helpless child that you and God created, that has been put in your care? Is he/she continually starving for your attention and affection? Are your kids (special-needs or not) becoming what you *really are?* And don't forget your grand kids; they will also model after you.

The bottom line is this: take care of your kids—especially the ones with special needs. In the process, they will see your modeling and consistency *and* for the most part adopt your value system. In my own case, I was the "runt of the litter" (not expected to live the first year nor to excel later) of nine children. But as things turned out, I was one of the two who lived near to help my parents as they grew old. This special child may be the one who takes care of you in your older years. In addition, who knows what impact your commitment to these children may have on your boss, co-workers, hired help, business suppliers, customers, friends and neighbors.

Finally, are you willing to forgo business expansion, professional advancement, recognition of your peers in whatever form, so your kids and especially your unpromising special-needs kids can be trained by you to walk with God? Or are you going to focus on your own "place in the sun" and let them slowly, emotionally and socially drown without your support? I am really sorry that I didn't start learning this until I was 45 or 50 years old.

Use Caution With "Professionals"

Another major point, let me scream it from the house top: *Don't be quick to turn your special child over to the "professional-social" caregivers.* Well-meaning people, clergy, friends, family and doctors may encourage you to do this or that "for your own good" or so the child can "reach his full potential." There are, I suppose, times when this may be true but I don't remember *any!* Keep in mind that *God gave this child to you, not to social services.* The special homes and social services cannot improve on the loving parent, no matter how much "apparent" skill they have. Keep in mind that many of these social services are funded by the number of bodies they can keep in their system.

In all fairness to the professionals, sometimes they rightly perceive that we are subconsciously looking for a way out of the difficult task that comes with the kind of commitment required to raise a child with special needs. It can be especially trying if we have a wrong view of children.

When we love our children and are committed to teaching and training them to leave behind the sometimes grody things that God hates; the proud look, the lying tongue etc.—there is satisfaction now and great rewards hereafter. Will you, will we cooperate?

Apart from the choices we all have to make, if our child turns out badly, we are held accountable. If our child does well, we deserve the credit. God keeps the books.

CHAPTER ELEVEN
What About My Normal Kids?

Ephesians 6:4
"And you, fathers, do not provoke your children to wrath but bring them up in the training and admonition of the Lord."

Recognize That Your Normal Children Have Needs Too

If God had given us only one child and He chose that the child would be born with special needs, we could concentrate all our attention on him. As I have already mentioned, we have two other children. Nathan's physical needs demanded huge amounts of time. It was difficult to keep in perspective that our other two, who were four and six years older, also needed us. There were only so many hours in the day, how did we decide which came first? Sometimes we missed seeing the needs of our other two.

Eric started first grade in our village school three weeks after Nathan was born. Being shy and having an overbearing teacher his first year in school was very distressing for him. For disobedience she hit hands with a ruler and blew a whistle for attention. We were so busy with Nathan we didn't know how detrimental this was for Eric. As an answer to prayer for a better teacher, Mr. Pacey came that next year and Eric blossomed under his gentle teaching. I feel that Eric's acceptance of Nathan would have been much easier if we had been home educating and not pushed him out the door to a difficult school situation every morning.

Chris, being home with me every day until she started school two years later, had an improved situation. She was involved with Nathan's care every day. Being the middle child, she was usually the mediator between her two brothers. She was Eric's deputy sheriff in cowboys and Indians and Nathan's playmate and entertainer.

Although our older children didn't often complain, we know that there were many times that they wanted to do something or go somewhere that we couldn't because of Nathan's needs. Parents grow tired after a day at work or with the extra requirements of the child with special needs, leaving little energy for fun times as a family. Since we farm, we did have more flexibility than many families. Rainy days were our escape days.

Once, when Nathan's appointment to the Kansas Medical Center was postponed, we were packed for the four hour trip so we took the whole family to Minden, Nebraska to see the museum. That was a memorable time. Excursions like that were rare. Our vacations were more likely to be hikes on the creek or fishing trips. If I had that time to do over, I would have looked for short fun times with the other children. Depending on the disability, it is almost impossible to take long trips with a child who has special needs. Nathan didn't enjoy traveling or changes in routine, and once he was on the diabetic diet, it was difficult to leave him with one of the grandmothers. They didn't cook low calorie/no sugar and he loved to find all the cookies and candy they had available.

Since junior high school was so difficult emotionally for all our children, I am sure that a lot of the family problems came from frustration with peer relationships at school. No child can spend eight hours competing with their peers, ride the bus home, and have enough emotional resources to handle the stress of a special-needs brother or sister easily. I know after I have spent a day shopping, I am in no mood to be gentle with my children and to remember my priorities. But if we had spent the morning working on studies together and then taken the afternoon for field trips or hands-on projects, even with my impatient nature, I am almost sure relationships would have been better.

Other parents have noticed the difficulties of relationships between the special-needs child and their siblings.

Stephanie of Kansas is the oldest in her family and for a few years was the only one her mother home schooled. Selena said,

> *Our second child used to resent the extra attention that I gave Stephanie. She would ask why. I would explain why God allowed her to learn so quickly and not Stephanie. I would make a special effort to spend time with Kimberly one-on-one. Amber, the youngest, is very amiable and is bothered by hardly anything.*

I asked if home educating all the girls had helped the resentment. Selena said

> *The problem has been mostly resolved prior to home schooling; how-*

ever, character and personality traits have improved in all the girls with home schooling. Stephanie gets easily frustrated and doesn't know how to express it in an acceptable manner. She doesn't understand voice inflection and body language and how it affects what she says. Reasoning traits are poor.

A mother in Maryland said,

> Sometimes the other two (teenagers) children are understanding and sometimes they just need to talk. Home schooling has definitely helped, because it caused the family to form a tight bond. Therefore talking about the situation has become easier.

As Mary Ann in Kansas said, "Our older children feel that I treated our son special and that he was a spoiled baby. They are not close to him as they all have grown older." Mary Ann only home schooled Tyler because he was not making it through public school junior high. Her other children were grown by then.

Laura of Michigan said,

> Our two older children resent Gideon. He seems to get away with more because of his lack of understanding. He gets more attention because of his behavior. He is mean to them for no reason at times. I think public school would make it worse though. Siblings who attend public school get driven apart. We are trying to train our children to see the importance of a family unit, each is special and needed.

Jean of Kansas said that her autistic son plays well with his older and younger brothers but, "there are times when Tyler (age 9) needs to be by himself and totally unwind. During these times he is easily agitated by his brother."

Spend Special Time With the Normal Child

One or both parents need to make time to spend with their other children. It will go a long way to making our normal children feel special by explaining to them about the stress that it puts on the family when Mommy and Daddy have to spend so much time with the child who has special needs. They need to know that we appreciate all the help they have been and that we love them as much as the other children. Just a few minutes of time alone daily, if possible, with the normal child would go a long way to convince them that they are just as important as the child with special needs who requires so much of Mommy and Daddy's time.

Valerie of Massachusetts, found this to be true. She said that her four year old relates well with Megan who is eight.

> *We found it necessary to explain to Caitlin when she was 2½ years old that Megan has Down's Syndrome. She wanted to wear a diaper during nap time like Megan even though she had been sleeping through naps without being wet. Caitlin loves Megan dearly; they are each other's best friends. I think home schooling has helped their relationship because they are learning together. They have more time together than they would have if Megan (or both) were in public school. They have a lot of fun experiences together that wouldn't have happened otherwise.*

Evelyn of Kansas, mother of a daughter with special needs and herself a special-education teacher, said,

> *Our family is very close. My children relate well with each other. They help each other. Just this year, Nathan sent Kari a thank-you note after he graduated from college. It said, "I'm glad you're my sister. I'm looking forward to spending more time with you." Often Kari and Karyn will call each other, just to talk. Both Karyn and Nathan are very supportive of Kari.*

Kathy in Texas said of her Sarah, her second child who has Downs,

> *Raise your children with the same love and attention. Do not favor the child with the disability. Spend quality time with the child who needs you the most—the child who needs the education to live a productive life—"the normal" one. They actually need more! However, because I have over-responded to this "philosophy," it has led to a spoiled teenager who has learned to manipulate me. Keep a balance! Teach servanthood (and Robin is a good and capable, but sometimes reluctant servant) to all children.*

Sheila of North Carolina said that their other three children don't treat Katye, 8 years with epilepsy and learning problems, any different than they treat each other. "I'm sure home schooling has fostered a love for each other that would not have been otherwise."

Randon of Kansas who was born with Prader-Willi Syndrome, as our son was, is protected by his older brother, Tyler, a year older at 8. He walks Randon to school each day. They share a room, they play together. Cindy, his mother, said,

> I haven't seen any embarrassment or being ashamed of his brother. They get along very well. The youngest loves his older brother dearly because he is so happy and fun to play with. He takes responsibility which he normally wouldn't have to do if Randon didn't have special needs.

No matter how well adjusted our normal child seems, they need to know that they also are unique and loved by us parents. If it doesn't work to do spur-of-the moment outings for the whole family, take turns spending extra time with the normal child, one at a time. Let them be children without always having to look out for their brother or sister. Just because they are uncomplaining doesn't mean they don't resent always being the one who does extra chores or helps with the care giving. We all need time to be ourselves and unwind from pressures.

Teach Your Normal Children About Their Special-Needs Siblings

I don't remember spending much time teaching our older children about Nathan's difficulties of having Preder Willi Syndrome. If we had explained more about why Nathan couldn't control his eating (because he lacked part of the 15th chromosome) and clarified why Nathan always felt hungry, it might have helped. But no sibling appreciates finding out that his brother has eaten all the cookies in the house.

Rosalie from Kansas came up with an excellent solution. She said,

> Home education has been invaluable in all our family relationships. Our children have been each others' classmates for thirteen years and have learned to get along with each other. Incorporating Harmony (with Downs) into the family was a "natural." Since Harmony had congestive heart failure, we adjusted our curriculum to accommodate her needs. We studied the heart and lungs and reviewed the CPR course that we had taken a few years earlier. We also studied books on Down's Syndrome as well as basic infant care booklets. Making her a _part_ of our curriculum really helped. The children were all trained to meet her needs and no one felt that she was a hindrance to "school."

Heather in South Carolina has five older brothers and sisters who have all been home schooled. Fay, her mother, also found ways to include their normal children. She said,

> Our older children have been a real help to Heather over the years. We have all treated her as if she were normal, including her in everything that was going on. They have helped teach her in school at times. Only three of them remain living close to home but they are still including her in their activities, taking her places and doing things with her. They do not apologize to anyone for her. They just love her and care for her as their sister. They do on occasion have to interpret her speech to someone if they do not understand her.

Parents hold the key to seeing that the needs of their normal children are met while giving much time and effort to their special-needs child. Part of meeting the needs of the normal children may be planning spur-of-the moment excursions as a family or family night events. Another possibility could be asking grandparents if they live near you, to take the normal children for a special time together. Both sets of our parents lived within four miles of us while the children were growing up. Our children were welcome in their homes any time. I didn't realize how much time our children spent with the grandparents until I read through my journal. That was a real blessing that I sort of took for granted. After reading that, I called my parents to thank them for being available.

If you don't have parents living near you, as many families don't, "adopt" a grandparent from your church or neighborhood. There are many lonely senior citizens whose own grandchildren live out-of-state, who might enjoy visiting with your normal children. There are many ways you could initiate this visiting which would be excellent training for your child. I would enjoy having a young neighbor child come for a visit since our own grandchildren live three to ten hours from our farm.

Terry and Robert of Maryland said that their two older children are excited when their eight year old adopted son with Downs learns something new. Terry said,

> I think that home schooling has definitely been a factor in them being close to him, the same way it has given them opportunity to be closer to each other. They have all been spared the pain of being ridiculed due to Stephen having Down's Syndrome. They know Stephen is as important as any other person! They also take part in home schooling Stephen. They read to him, tell him stories and help him with skills

like counting while setting the table.

Since there are no mistakes in God's program, the special-needs child may have been placed in the family so that the other children will learn some practical lessons which they will need later in life. Look for ways to teach them how to relate to those who are not mentally and/or physically as capable as they are.

Rosalie said,

> All of our children think that Harmony is the best thing that has happened to our family. The older boys (25 and 24 years) come in the door and sweep her up into their arms and talk to her. The girls and younger son help to teach and train her. The older girls often care for her when I need to be away from the home although I sometimes hire a sitter.

Su of Wisconsin said that Ben's older and younger siblings have been most supportive and have encouraged him in every step. He was the only one that she home schooled.

Sandy of New York told about Sarah, who was adopted,

> Since our children were all grown by the time we started home schooling, there hasn't been any problem with them. They do ask us all the time how we do it—like some insurmountable task. You just DO it! The ones who ask that aren't serving the Lord though, and that makes a big difference. The ones who are, completely agree with home schooling and either are or plan to home school their own.

Debbie of Kansas, who didn't start home educating Travis until he was nine said of his relationship with his brother and sister,

> Trish has always "mothered" Travis. There are only two years age difference. They work very well together. Tim has always been an independent learner and could achieve greater tasks than others his age, at 17, he was a second semester sophomore in college and national honor student.

Lane from Kansas with multiple handicaps has an older sister and two younger foster siblings. Carol, his mother, said,

> He will relate when HE feels like it, not when we initiate it. Our two youngest are seven and eight and in the last couple of years have

learned skills that Lane has spent years learning. I think they now understand better how limited Lane's understanding is as they progress past him. They do a few things like read to him (very occasionally), tickle, wrestle around, chase after the basketball when he throws it. They don't really respond any differently except they have had to learn to be more careful with him physically so as not to have him fall and get injured (due to his poor balance and the rod in his back). Again, he prefers to spend a lot of time to himself. He prefers talking to adults who usually take time to listen and try to understand what he is saying and doing. This is a weakness. I wish he had peers to spend time with.

His sister, Christy, 19 years, is training in physical therapy. She has worked with Lane often during his growing up.

Karen, a pastor's wife in Kansas, said,

My girls act like very normal sisters. They fight, they share, they compete against each other. Katherine sometimes resents having to help Christine but that is entirely normal. Katherine is a very sensitive child and picks up on the times I (mom) need help, like walking down a dark sidewalk. But then she resents having to walk all over town instead of driving because Mom can't see. Overall, I think our vision difficulty is just a part of our lives. The girls, at this time, treat it very naturally.

Jane in Oregon wrote,

It isn't easy to grow up in a family of potentially explosive, "different" brothers, as was the case with our family until Joy, our oldest daughter, was ten years old. Nevertheless, again the knowledge that God planned her also and that she is special to me has helped. Early in her life, Joy was very quiet and shy yet has always had her father's Irish wit and known just how and when to use it. I would say that growing up with these brothers seems to have strengthened Joy's life rather than weakened it. She has a very compassionate, non-judgmental spirit which holds her in good stead as a pastor's wife. (Joy is now the mother of three daughters.)

As a bit of advice, if there was any shortcoming in Joy's early life, it was getting her share of my time. Because she was so capable, it was easy to let her fend for herself. The boys took so much time and needed still more. I was very blessed to have Christian friends who realized this need and would take Joy for special afternoon and visits. I think that the need *of the siblings of a special-needs child is a close relationship with someone outside the immediate family.*

Linda from Minnesota told about their adopted son, who is several years younger than their three daughters. She said,

> *Our daughters have always treated him as if he did not have a disability, more than we have. The girls are often frustrated by his teasing. The older two girls have become skilled trainers and enjoy learning child psychology. His nearest sibling had a difficult time adjusting to the extra attention he receives.*

They had been home educators four years before adopting their son.

From our own experience and what I have learned from the other families, I know that open communication with the other siblings is absolutely necessary to inform as well as assure the normal child that they are just as important to you as the special-needs child. The home education situation works well to incorporate the normal children in learning to accept and care for their special-needs sibling. This is excellent training for life. As several parents mentioned, they used materials about the disability as part of their education, another daughter learned physical therapy while working with her brother while other daughters learned psychology while working with their little brother.

Just as God uses the special-needs child in the lives of the parents, He also teaches lessons on acceptance and right attitude about that special-needs brother or sister to prepare the siblings to work and accept all people regardless of ability.

CHAPTER TWELVE
Parents Have Special Needs Also

> *Ephesians 5:33*
> *"Nevertheless let each one of you in particular so love his own wife as himself, and let the wife see that she respects her husband."*

Cherish Your Wife—Respect Your Husband

Nathan's physical and mental problems put a lot of stress on our marriage especially after he started to school. We usually agreed on other decisions but when it came to Nathan's problems we could violently disagree. I thought Nathan should be pushed harder; Ellis thought we should be more patient. I thought we should just insist that he stay out of food and force him to obey; Ellis thought we should reason with him. He would say, "Let me talk to him about it." When the stress became too difficult for me, I would push Ellis to do something, anything, to straighten out Nathan. I thought we should use force to keep Nathan from continuing to gain weight and wrecking his health.

The only way we could agree on what to do was to pray together over the problem, seeking God's wisdom. Almost every night we would pray before going to sleep and we still do. When we both sought God's plan, we began finding the answers that God had for us. Early in our marriage Matthew 6:33 had become a key verse, "But seek ye first the kingdom of God and His righteousness and all these things shall be added unto you." Having that as a base puts decisions in a different perspective. It isn't what I want done or what Ellis wants done but what God had planned for Nathan and for us. God gave Nathan to us so He knew the whole plan for Nathan even before he was born. We needed to fit into that plan. It was not always easy but once we sought God's plan surprising things happened. I was often too impatient to wait for God's wisdom.

While trying to decide on having the surgery to fuse Nathan's vertebra, we found that we could take him to the specialist at Loma Linda in

California during the time we were at a family reunion. This sounded good to me because I like the idea of traveling. Ellis hates to travel even to see family. We *strongly* "*discussed*" this for several weeks. I couldn't see why it wouldn't work out and Ellis couldn't see why we should go. Finally after talking to his brother, who had made the appointment with the doctor, he decided that we would go. What we learned from that doctor prevented us from putting Nathan through serious major surgery. And Ellis almost enjoyed visiting with his family—the only time he has been to California to visit them.

The relationship between a husband and wife must be on sound footing before children arrive. A child with special needs puts stress on the relationship. Now I don't delight in the word *submission,* but once I saw that my submission to Ellis was really submission to Christ that helped. Someone has to make the final decisions and God said that was to be the husband's role. I am not naturally a quiet submissive person so decisions concerning Nathan were the times we had some of our worst disagreements.

Respect is another word given in Scripture for wives. It is an entirely different word; it means that you honor, admire, esteem, have a high opinion of, appreciate, have high regard, prize, value. Now wouldn't any husband love a wife who thought highly of him. No husband should say, "if she will respect me, I will love her." Nor should a wife say, "If he will love me, I will respect him." It is a matter of *will,* not what the other spouse does or doesn't do in fulfilling the Biblical role.

Satan attacks where we are weakest and he doesn't like to see strong marriages. We give him an opening by allowing problems to remain unsettled at the end of each day and not seeking forgiveness from our spouse and/or children. There are several areas that help prevent problems from becoming impossible. One is communication between husband and wife.

Tom Holiman, Executive director of Arkansas Christian Home Education Assoc. Wrote, "Because the home-school movement is primarily a spiritual movement producing a strong grassroots revival across this land, we had better prepare ourselves for the spiritual battle to follow."

He continues,

> What good will it do to be successful in courts and legislatures across this country if our families are in disarray? How will we indeed take on persecution if our marriages are failing? What have we accomplished? I strongly feel this is where Satan is persecuting us now. He is attacking home schoolers at the heart of their families—marriage itself....[1]

Marilyn, from Pennsylvania, said, "When both mates accept this from the Lord, stress is minimal as you go to God for wisdom and strength daily."

We attended a family seminar on marriage while our children were quite young. One key point that has stuck with me through the years was the list of *priorities* for a married couple:

1. Your relationship to God
2. You relationship to your spouse
3. Your relationship to your children
4. Your work/job responsibilities
5. Your ministry/outreach into the community

Sometimes the decision isn't black and white but it helps tremendously to remember that you must be in a right relationship with God before you can relate well with your spouse and in a right relationship with your spouse before you can relate well with the children. If your association with the Lord, your spouse and/or your children isn't right, your job or ministry will be affected.

Children will take just as much time as you will give out and more if you don't teach them the limits. Finding that balance, especially with a child who has special needs with many physical and/or mental problems is not easy but must be done.

It is easy to be so tied up with the child's every day needs that you don't talk through the problems with your spouse. You must talk in order to work as a team. Find time during the day for a few minutes alone to talk. *Children can be taught that Mom and Dad need time alone and to not interrupt unless it is an emergency.*

Other parents also said that raising a special-needs child put stress on their marriage. Here are some of their observations:

Sandy, of New York, who adopted blind and profoundly retarded Sarah, after having five children of their own, said,

> *I can see how the stress could be felt if the responsibility is not shared between husband and wife. It can seem to be a burden if there is not respite for both parents. Moms, dads and the other children need to lead a somewhat normal life style. Kids need to play ball and have Mom and Dad there to watch, even if their special brother and sister can't be outside that long. I think it is important for parents to have time alone. We are fortunate to have public health respite paid for by Medicaid which*

followed Sarah at her adoption. My husband and I take Fridays from 12-5 p.m. to do shopping, errands and go out to lunch. There are still some days when I wish I could just get in the car and come back when I'm ready to instead of when the nurse is scheduled to leave. But my husband is always willing to stay home so I can roam in the mall or spend hours in the fabric store. I encourage him to go fishing when the weather permits. Our spare time is limited but we don't really feel "stressed" as I hear some parents say.

Kathy, of Texas, wrote,

> In all of this which has happened, the Lord has brought me to Him because my marriage is insufficient—my relationship with my husband is suffering, has been suffering. We will have our 21st anniversary in October. Not celebrating or rejoicing, but groaning in agony over the weight of the circumstances, the weight of the years. We do not handle the stress. We struggle along allowing it to overwhelm us. Right now I cannot "rise above" the crisis of our daughter. The problem comes from my husband and I not committing our marriage to God. When the marriage is not "whole," healthy, the children will not be raised in a healthy environment or manner. I do not feel the victory today. I do not rejoice. I know I should count all this as joy, because He is perfecting me. I need to fall in love again with my Savior and Lord.

You Must Find Time to Communicate

The communication is necessary to prevent minor problems from becoming major. One mother suggested that you set a certain time for bed for the special-needs child so the evening can be spent with your spouse. These are areas that you need to agree on and work together to implement them.

Marsha, from Missouri, shared,

> Yes, it is stressful raising our daughter with spina bifida and hydrocephalus but the key is to be best friends with your spouse. This can only be done if God is put first. And it requires constant communication with each other, which is sometimes very difficult, because the fatigue level goes up with the stress level. Say, "I love you" to each other several times a day. Hugs are great too!

Sheila, from North Carolina, who has two special-needs children, said that talking out their fears, concerns, praises and problems is the best way to lower stress. "We both have hobbies we can bury ourselves in—his is computers and mine is handcrafts. We also have time alone."

Jackie, of Colorado, said,

> We have not had the stress of any physical therapy to attend all the time. We do have to see different specialists regularly to keep abreast of the latest developments in the medical field and then make the decision if these are a wise choice for Christopher. We will have the stress of many operations and with the possibility of him dying at the back of our minds all his life. We just get through the days by trying to accomplish what needs to be done. My husband is not involved in the doctor visits or daily grind for Christopher, but all decisions are a joint agreement. Our only _hope_ is in the Lord. Without Him everything would be useless. We know all our children will be perfect in the Lord's presence.

Laura of Michigan, whose third child has special needs, said,

> Sure it's stressful. Sometimes, at any given time, either my husband or I feel the other one is being too hard or too soft on Gideon. We don't always agree on what should be done concerning his education, discipline, sleeping arrangements, etc. (He hates to sleep alone.) Then we'll disagree about the other children and how Gideon relates to them. We deal with the stress by talking. (Yelling if we have to.) My sister and her husband never talk. They have a moderately retarded son. Her husband will go for days without speaking to her. That's wrong. My sister hears my husband and me disagreeing and she freaks out thinking our marriage is over. She is very far from the truth.
>
> No, I don't condone screaming matches but honest communication is a must. A parent has to have someone on their side, if not the other parent then who? And I hate to say this but wives have to allow their husband in as fathers of these kids. Spending 24 hours a day with _my_ kids, I get protective. It's not easy to allow some big, selfish man to take over whenever he feels like it. But God is trustworthy. He's completing the work in our husband just as He is in us. We have to trust our children to their father's hands. God is able. Amen.

Lonnie, the father of Lane, of Kansas, said to help with the stress, he helps around the house. He said, "She doesn't get out a lot. The first five or six years with Lane (after she quit her good paying job to care for him) there was no money for dates so we would take Lane with us grocery shopping and eating out." They couldn't afford a nurse to care for him and babysitters were afraid to try it especially after his back surgery. Now they have a baby sitter for the two younger children and Lane gets along all right that way.

Find Stress Relievers

Often during the spring, summer and fall, Ellis would come to the door and ask, "Want to go for a walk?" He knew that I had a hectic day with Nathan who was determined to eat everything in the house. I would grab a jacket and we would walk in the pasture across the road or down along our grass field. That was when we did our talking but often we made the rule, "Don't talk about problems."

Ellis would remind me "Remember we only talk about the good things that happened today." It is so easy to focus only on the problems and we need to force ourselves to see there are blessings also. Nathan's screaming at me after he had eaten sweets made daily life difficult but walking off my aggravation gave a whole new perspective.

On one walk we saw three deer in the wheat field. In breathless silence we watched as they munched on the young green wheat. They bounded away with white tails flagging leaving us to laugh at the sight. The chatter of the birds and the flight of the pheasants as we walked along was healing. We came back refreshed ready to handle Nathan's problems again.

Not all families can leave their child alone but you need to arrange some time away even if you have to do it separately. Christ took time to get alone to pray and meditate away from people.

Not all parents that I interviewed felt that their special needs child added stress to their marriage. One mother from Maryland said,

> We try to have one night every month for dinner and time to communicate and to take this opportunity to reach out to others with similar situations. We try to remember that this is a season of life and each moment is precious. We are thankful to God for His faithfulness. Deuteronomy 33:24B "And your strength will equal your days."

Valerie, of Massachusetts, said,

> I guess raising a child is stressful to a marriage but I don't see that it has caused much stress in our marriage. Maybe we're strange or maybe God's working in our lives. Megan having Down's Syndrome was never much of a blow to us so maybe we're a little different than other people! Having Down's Syndrome is not the tragedy that some

people make it out to be. We do have the Lord in our lives so maybe that is the difference.

Fay, of North Carolina, is another one who said,

> *I guess most folks would call me a little odd, but I do not find it any more stressful raising a Down's Syndrome child than I did raising a "normal" child. Actually, Heather gives us less stress than the other children do right now. Even though our other five children are mostly adults, they're still our children. I guess as we grow older, we have more problems and this may prove true for Heather also. But, we treat Heather as if she were a normal child. Being home schooled, she is not around other people so much, so when she is, others look at her a little different and some stare, especially the older person. I find the younger the child the more willing they are to accept Heather for who and what she is and it doesn't bother them that she is different. Heather is really a sweet little girl. Doing very well in her school work, although very slow. She has no major problems. Her speech is very poor and we have to do a lot of interpreting. But the more a person is around her the more they understand what she is saying. Of course there are a few minor things that concern us, such as bed wetting, chewing with her mouth open when she eats, not sitting properly for a young lady, etc., but overall I believe these things will change as she grows older. When I think of it, I believe our other children had the same problems when they were young. They learned how to handle the situations and I'm sure Heather will too. Without our daily praying for God's leading and wisdom in all the matters of daily living, our day would be filled with stress. But, passing it on to the Lord in Heaven to do His will relieves us of tremendous stress. And anyhow, that's what He wants us to do. We do have the tendency to worry, but then realizing that worry is sin because it's not trusting in God fully, and exercising our faith in Him, we come to realize that it's all going to work out to be whatever God wants in our lives.*

Ginia, of Maryland, wrote,

> *I don't necessarily think Andrew having Down's Syndrome stressed us out any more than the stress that comes with just having another child. For the most part, we both feel the same. When I tell my husband that I don't feel right about something and I'm not sure why, he doesn't ask any questions, he just stands by me 100%. We pray. My husband is*

more medically oriented and knowledgeable so when we had medical problems to face—he "screened" them and "took charge."

Terry and Robert, of Maryland, said,

> Knowing that God had a reason for Stephan being on this earth and a reason for him being a part of our family helps us with the stress. We also have a lot of family support because everyone loves and accepts him as he is.

Janice, of Kansas, said,

> My husband Geoff is my balance rod. He is more calm, where I tend to be emotional. At a seminar we both attended, he heard a home schooling father (who was also a pastor) share the father's role in the decision making and re-enforcing the mother. He does that for me, helping me to keep focused and acting as the principal of our home school. This way I am accountable to him and the children know they are also. I ask him for input in areas that I might be struggling with. Together we set goals for each year. He observes the children and helps me determine where they are struggling and suggests what we might change to accommodate that particular need. He also helps balance me spiritually, so that I don't get too wrapped up in the here and now, losing sight of the eternal goal. It is really easy to get tunnel vision when you are immersed in daily routines.

I think Janice hit on an important principle—her husband is head of the family—helping to keep her on focus. That was our goal in our family. Even though we didn't always agree, Ellis made the final decisions after we had discussed or argued through the problems. That in itself is stress relieving. If I don't have to convince Ellis that my plan for the problem is the right one, that gives him freedom to make the decision. The husband is accountable to God, not the wife for his decisions. If he makes a mistake—never, never say, "I told you so." God will make him aware of that.

Mary, of Indiana, said, "Yes, it adds stress to our marriage, but it also teaches better communication skills between each other and the Lord."

Linda, of Minnesota, said,

> Yes, we have found parenting a child with special needs stressful to family life and to our marriage, but we are committed to laying down

our lives for this little one God has given. When I was pregnant with our firstborn, God gave me scriptural song that I have felt was confirmed in our sons's addition to our family: unto us a child is born, unto us a son is given. He's the promise of the Father, who reigns in highest Heaven. He was born not after the flesh, but according to the Spirit. God gives. God gives.

Linda also gave several suggestions at a seminar on *Meeting the Challenge of Unique Learning Needs*. She suggested adequate rest, taking turns, natural supports, county services, meditation and music, fresh air and light.

Jane, from Oregon, wrote,

> Yes, it is very stressful to a marriage to have a special-needs child. I don't have exact statistics, but the divorce rate of parents of autistic children is 70-80%. What advice would I give to maintain a healthy marriage? I will list them:
>
> A. Keep your spiritual life strong. Stay in the word and maintain your prayer life. This helps everyone cope with stress.
>
> B. Allow each other to grieve. As I said earlier, grief will be there and not everyone will grieve in the same way. Learn to recognize these times of grief in each other and allow for it. If you are having a question about this one, a good Christian family counselor can be invaluable here.
>
> C. If there is any secret to my marriage of 26 years, it is that my husband has taught me to laugh. We get silly and we get corny at times, but if you cannot see the humor in life, you are lost. I think that laughter is one of the healthiest of all positive responses. As someone has said, there is joy in the journey. Learn to spot it and savor it.
>
> D. Another thing Roy has brought to our marriage is an amazing ability to "wing it." We don't always know exactly what we are doing, but we aren't afraid to step in and try.
>
> E. All of this is a part of what I would call hanging loose. If you are too tight and regimented and expect too much perfection out of a given situation, and if you set up this type of lifestyle around a handicapped child, it will drive you crazy because, "it just ain't a gonna be that way" and no matter how much you try, you will not achieve your goal.

F. Lastly, learn to focus on your mate and your marriage. If one or the other partner become too possessed by the overwhelming needs of the special-needs child and forgets that his mate has needs too, soon the marriage is in trouble, and that is definitely unhealthy for the child who is receiving the out-of- balance focus. Roy and I date alone, at least once every two weeks. Dates don't have to cost a lot. It is just that you must find some time to give each other undivided attention and communication. Christian friends can be invaluable here if they recognize that you have this need. They may give you a bit of respite by keeping your children for you even for a very short time. You might even offer this gift to another couple in exchange for keeping your kids.

Secular studies agree with Jane on humor. At a women's meeting they read this to us,

Laughter is a stress reducer. When a person laughs, he or she briefly loses muscle tone. All the tense muscles of the body are relaxed. Some physicians find they can cure tension headaches by getting patients to laugh. Humor gives us the ability to laugh or make fun of something serious therefore helping release tension. Humor helps a person to cope with the trying circumstances by substituting a frame of mind that is incompatible with anxiety or distress. One cannot be playful and worried at the same time. If a person has been involved in conflict for any length of time, it will be difficult for that person to be flexible enough to appreciate playful thoughts, so humor needs to be established early in the conflict. Humor can represent cognitive mastery. We can learn from a previously painful event and may actually be able to laugh at it later. (Author unknown)

Several families said that they made a special effort to have an evening out together and to hire a babysitter so they could do this. We had two grandmothers within 4 miles who were willing to take care of our children for a few hours until Nathan's diabetes made him insulin dependent. That made our outings more difficult to schedule.

Sharon, of British Columbia, told of the dates that she and Gerry have had while raising their two adopted sons with Downs and their older daughter. Gerry has had Multiple sclerosis for several years which forced him to cut back on his work hours but he was still able to work until March of 1995.

He fell while at work landing on his head which paralyzed him from the neck down. He was hospitalized in Vancouver for almost a year. Sharon plans on him being home full time as soon as their home can be remodeled to be wheel-chair accessible. His van has been adapted so that he can drive once his health problems improve. Once or twice during his hospitalization they were able to go on a date in Vancouver.

Another mother felt that giving specific prayer requests to friends helped them survive the rough times. Selena said, "I guess just pouring my heart out to God often helps keep the stress from accumulating."

Some mothers are able to leave the children with their father while they shop or visit a friend. Look for ways that will fit into your budget and time schedule to give each caregiver time away to relieve the stress.

A bow constantly stretched will break. Every couple has to work out what fits best in their situation and change it as the care of their child changes. Each of the parents I interviewed came up with some excellent practical advice: time with the Lord, time to communicate, pray about the problems, look for brief times to get away and learn to laugh— "merry heart does good like a medicine." Proverbs 17:22.

My husband's family is known for their humor and my husband inherited that ability. Family humor creates memories for the children. Nathan loved to tease and laugh with us. He didn't always understand all the family jokes but he did make lots of his own. Ellis encouraged our laughter by funny stories or jokes.

One evening when we were feeling especially stressed, we read in the paper that there was a good comedy movie at the theater. We hired a baby sitter and spent the evening laughing. There is something about a good laugh that removes the tight stressful feelings.

I have always spent much time outside digging in the dirt, and seeing plants green up and grow, the better my emotions and physical health become. I always start my day in God's Word, even when I don't feel like it, God gives me a blessing but being outside, seeing His creation and feeling the sunshine, is when I began to rebuild my inner being.

There are trials in every marriage. Children add to those trials especially the child with special physical and mental needs. Our response to those comes from our relationship with God and with our spouse.

"A Merry Heart Doeth Good Like A Medicine"

Nathan and Ellis shared lots of laughs as they rode in the pickup around the farm. When Nathan was eleven, Ellis was discussing something he wanted Nathan to do and Nathan was resisting. Ellis asked, "Who's the boss in this pickup?" Nathan immediately answered, "No one!"

As husbands cherish their wives and wives respect their husbands and together they give God's plan first place in their family, they will find ways to relieve the stress of raising a special-needs child. A support group (preferably Christian) where you can share prayer requests, a prayer partner, exercise and time alone help make the stress bearable. Look for opportunities for a good laugh with your child and your spouse. "A merry heart does good like a medicine."

NOTES:

[1] *The Teaching Home*, July/Aug 1994, Guest Editorial, "Warning to Home Schoolers!" P.O. Box 12311, Portland, OR 97230.

CHAPTER THIRTEEN
The Future, Where, When and What?

Proverbs 29:18
"Where there is no vision
(revelation from God)
the people perish...."

Have a Plan for the Future of Your Special-Needs Child

Once Nathan made it through high school at almost 20 years of age, we breathed a sigh of relief. That was a major accomplishment. We knew he wasn't college material but hoped that he could work in a local library or museum using his love and knowledge of books and research. We really didn't know what he could physically or mentally handle or how to go about planning his future. We were relieved that we had survived 12 years of schooling and that he was keeping his weight sort of under control. I don't remember planning anything any further at that time.

Not long after high school, Nathan talked of finding an apartment in town. We didn't take him seriously as we knew that he couldn't do his own cooking or stay on his diabetic meals without supervision. He had been on a diabetic diet since 7th grade to help keep his weight down but also because sugar altered his thinking.

Since he enjoyed studying, he and I took several Junior college night classes together. We took one class a semester but Nathan took one that I didn't. He took Bible as Literature that our pastor taught, and did quite well with it. We both took geography and enjoyed the teacher who talked on everything except the subject and gave open book tests. If he wasn't rushed, Nathan could do the work and passed his tests. We both took a semester class called *Learning Special Education* which gave the public schools' view of teaching special-needs children.

We felt Nathan should help at home, so he did the push mowing of our large acreage. He needed the exercise and didn't mind hours of mowing. We had tried a riding mower but his back couldn't stand the rough ride. We gave him an allowance for helping in this way. Sometimes he would drive the pickup as Ellis moved the tractor to the field. This relieved me of picking him up from the field and gave Nathan the job of helping. Nathan had taken drivers education in school and passed it to receive his license. The educational psychologist had told us several years before that he *never* would be able to accomplish that. It seemed like the experts were always wrong about Nathan.

The winter before Nathan turned 23, he insisted that he was moving to town immediately. We started looking into supervised group homes in towns within 50 miles. Some were so bad that we wouldn't even consider them and none had any provision to keep food from being too available for him. We finally opted for the Elkhorn Senior citizen/handicapped home in Minneapolis. They had a live-in supervisor and it was near the doctor/dentist clinic. They had an opening and the payments were set up according to Nathan's income so we could afford it.

Soon after Nathan moved to his apartment, we were told by SSI that he could be tested for a job ability and probably receive SSI benefits for his disability so we scheduled those. We both wish that we had never agreed to this. Nathan had been functioning well in his apartment for several weeks. He would drive to the hospital for his noon meal and to the museum to work a few hours in the little Datsun car we found for him.

The testing that Nathan was to receive was to be for 5 days 9 a.m. to 3 p.m. We took him to Salina to talk to the supervisor of the testing place, Kansas Vocational Rehabilitation Center. We told them that he was allergic to sugar and that he did not function well if he had it. The supervisor said they would make sure that he didn't receive sugar. We found a ride for him from Minneapolis with a young Christian man who worked near the testing facilities. Nathan made it through the first two days but he called the third day to say he wasn't sure he could handle going again. Ellis talked him into going but we didn't realize that he was becoming over stressed. We did this over the phone which didn't give us a real idea of his stress.

The supervisor called after he arrived to say that Nathan seemed to be running a temperature so I gave permission to give him an aspirin. Evidently they pushed him hard all the rest of the day insisting that he do all they asked before they would let him stop at 3 p.m. The minute Nathan finished the testing he tried to find the supervisor but could not so he walked out into the 95 degree day. He told me later that he had planned to walk to the library (he didn't know that it was 2 miles away) but instead he ended up on the interstate begging for a ride. A Minneapolis high school bus driver was delivering students home from a track meet and saw him out there and called me.

Nathan told us later that a truck driver picked him up and took him to a gas station where he called the girl who rode with them to Salina. She had the police come pick him up because the testing facility people and police had been looking all over town for him.

The nurse at KVRC called us to say they couldn't release him until they talked to us. She said that Nathan was okay and they were giving him some diet pop. She wanted to know if they should bring him home or did I want to pick him up. She told me that the police had brought him back. I told her that I would come.

Once I arrived I could see that he was *not* okay. He had lost his glasses and his shoes in his two hour walk in the heat. The young man who had provided his ride found his back pack in the parking lot of Tony's Pizza several blocks away.

Nathan talked incoherently most of the way back to his apartment about things he had seen on his walk. I heated him some supper and he sadly waved from his balcony when I left. Ellis called him later to find him still sounding very discouraged so he asked our co-pastor to visit him. Rob came and read the Bible to him until he fell asleep.

Nathan told us later that he thought they had given him sugar because he couldn't think and when the supervisor wasn't available at 3 p.m., he just walked out.

We had just fallen asleep after the distressing day. The phone rang at 11:30 p.m. It was our daughter who lives near Kansas City. She told us that their 8 month old daughter who had spinal muscular atrophy had just died. We had known since she was five months old that she wasn't well, but this was extra difficult on top of Nathan's problems.

The next morning Nathan called so we told him about Elise dying and then asked our pastor to prepare Nathan to leave with us to be with our daughter and her family. Nathan was so jumpy that he could hardly ride. Normally he slept as we traveled but he couldn't sleep. Everything upset him; he kept begging the whole three hours for us to take him back to his apartment. We couldn't leave him alone nor did we know of anyone where we could leave him.

Once at our daughter's home, our 4-year-old granddaughter, Erin, started "doctoring" Nathan with her little doctor's kit while our son-in-law told us about Elise's last hours. As we talked, Erin did much to bring Nathan out of his confusion. Somehow we made it through the burial and memorial service. Nathan slowly came out of his stress but if we had know what the tests involved we would never have had him tested. It wasn't worth the emotional trauma it put him through just to get a monthly check.

Once back home, we called up KVRC to talk about the tests. They were very apologetic. I am sure they thought we would sue them for their neglect of Nathan's health problems and not supervising him when he left the building. They rushed the results through so that Nathan was soon receiving a monthly check which paid for his room along with some extras. He had his own checking account even though he didn't understand much about money.

After 6 months in the apartment where Nathan gained almost 40 pounds, we became alarmed that his health was not good. One day it dawned on me that something was seriously wrong. I called the clinic to see if they could run tests. I called Nathan about his appointment at the clinic but he wasn't responding normally. I finally convinced him to walk over there. They found his blood sugar so high that it wouldn't register on their machine. The nurses told him to drive to the hospital to test on the machine there. It was 712 and you can go into a coma at 500. They immediately entered him into the hospital and started potassium and insulin injections and called us. From then on Nathan was on injected insulin. That was the beginning of several hospitalizations for Nathan as his health began to deteriorate.

Nathan stayed in the apartment from April until February of the next year. We knew he wasn't doing well there. Late on the coldest night of the year the supervisor called us to ask us to take Nathan home. The little old ladies had been feeding him candy which didn't help his disposition. He became irritable from the sugar and was complaining to one of the unpredictable ones. She called the supervisor who asked us to take Nathan home.

Our senior pastor thought that we should have some life of our own and should find a place where Nathan could be on his own. Nathan stayed with us until April while we looked into a group home near Wichita where all food was locked up and they had close supervision.

Nathan agreed to live at the home and while we were driving to Valley Center to enter him, he sang *Peace in the Valley* to us and thanked us for being good parents.

Most of the residents in the home were mentally behind Nathan. There was another resident who had Prader-Willi Syndrome. He took an immediate disliking to Nathan. Nathan became upset because he could call us only twice a month, so the boy with Prader-Willi suggested that Nathan cut the screen and escape out the window. Nathan did late one summer night.

After being called by the home at two in the morning with the report that Nathan had run away and that the police were out looking for him, we spent the rest of the night praying. They never did find him. He rode his bike which he had taken with him and hid in the ditches when cars came by until he arrived at the Kansas Coliseum which was five or six miles from the group-home. At eight in the morning he called us from a pay phone asking to come home. We called the supervisor who rushed to take him back for his insulin shots. They tried hard to meet his needs but Nathan was miserable there. He stayed another few weeks before the home supervisor asked us to take him some place for evaluation because of his temper outbursts. We took him right to Charter hospital in Wichita for 26 days of evaluation in early June.

While Nathan was in Charter, our oldest son and his wife took us to Colorado to visit her parents following our June wheat harvest. They must have known how much we needed that time away from emergencies with Nathan. We hiked the mountains and slept in every morning. Seeing God's wonderful creation in the mountains did so much to revive our inner being. I would sit in the porch swing each morning with the humming birds flying around the feeder, while I looked out over Methodist mountain and read God's word.

We brought Nathan home to stay in July. Charter hospital had come to the conclusion that he needed to be on Lithium (an anti-depressant) full time and a different insulin. Nathan had suffered much from his time away from us but he slowly recovered his mental balance but his physical condition would never be the same. Our oldest son said the following Christmas that he could see Nathan was slowly losing physical abilities.

Once Nathan recovered some mentally and physically, he started visiting at our small local hospital and making friends with the patients there for treatment from head injuries. That was the time the administrator asked if he would teach a Bible study to the head injury patients. He did teach them several weeks but couldn't handle the stress of their arguments. Nathan continued to visit the head injury patients often. He had the patience to listen to their garbled speech. If they couldn't talk, he told them what he was doing, sang or read Scripture to them.

While lithium did much to prevent the temper outbursts, which are not uncommon with Prader-Willi children, it had to be monitored regularly. Gradually we had to increase the amount because the small dose wouldn't work. After 5 years on Lithium, the psychiatric doctor said that we could look into changing his medication to see if that would help control him for a couple of weeks for them to regulate the change because he was becoming more difficult to handle.

As we signed papers to enter him, they asked "Do you care if Nathan attends some classes we offer?" We agreed that it would be okay but I kept having an uneasy feeling about the whole place and changing his medication. One of the classes, we found out later, was for patients who had tried to take their life with medicine. One girl with whom Nathan became friends, had tried to take her life with Lithium. After we had brought Nathan home, he told Ellis that it was wrong to take your life so we felt the class hadn't harmed him but after a month in the hospital we noticed that he wasn't functioning as well as he had before.

While still at the hospital, Nathan, who was always concerned about others, told us that he had talked to the doctor, asking him if he knew Jesus. He also wanted to give a Christian book to one of the patients so I purchased one for him to give her.

A few weeks before Nathan entered the hospital, we had purchased a 13 week old Chihuahua for him. We had heard from a dog breeder that Chihuahua's help with Asthma problems. Nathan was anxious to return home to his new puppy. That puppy slept snugly against Nathan's stomach every night and coaxed Nathan out of bed every morning. After a month they finally thought they had the new medication regulated so that he could be home. For awhile, life seemed more normal but we could see the new medication wasn't working. Nathan wasn't content and was easily irritated. He was on oxygen for several hours a day for his asthma problems.

In April, after he had been home six weeks or more, we asked him if he wanted to take a walk on the creek bank with us since it was a beautiful day. He said he wanted to take a nap with his puppy so we started his oxygen and drove four miles to the creek. Nathan didn't mind if we were gone a few hours.

Nathan's asthma had become worse. The week before, he had collapsed on the dining room table unable to get his breath after a coughing spell. I thought we had lost him then but with a cortisone shot and oxygen he revived.

We were gone probably 2 hours on our walk. As we drove in the drive, we heard a motor starting in the shed. That was unusual because we had no longer allowed Nathan to drive. We had taken his keys away because he wasn't emotionally able to handle driving. Before we knew what was happening, Nathan roared out of the yard with our car. Ellis jumped into the pickup to follow but Nathan was traveling so fast that he lost him in the dust.

Ellis came back to tell me that he couldn't find him. I had just noticed Nathan's old bottle of Lithium (which he was no longer taking) was empty along with the medication he was now taking. That was when we called 911 to seek help in finding him and to call the hospital to tell them what he had taken.

People all over the county were looking for him. Police, sheriff deputies and even a helicopter were looking. We were afraid he might have driven to Salina where we had never allowed him to drive. Our church prayer chain was praying. Two hours later, a cousin happened to think that Nathan might have gone to the Adee homestead (7 miles from our farm) which was abandoned. He and another cousin drove there and found Nathan and his little puppy sitting in the car. Nathan talked to them and was able to walk to the ambulance but by the time we arrived at the hospital he wasn't able to talk. He knew Ellis when he talked to him and seemed to say he was sorry for causing us problems.

They worked on him in emergency and ICU all night but there was nothing they could do. God took him to his heavenly home April 5, 1992 at the age of 27. We were surrounded by our Christian friends and relatives. God gave us the strength through the next rough days.

The church was packed for the memorial service. Nathan had touched so many lives in our small town. A classmate who had been into the occult and drugs came to the services because Nathan had befriended him following the boy's near fatal accident.

Store clerks who had waited on him, nurses at the hospital, people from all walks of life heard about Nathan's Lord and Savior. The last Sunday Nathan was at church, he had requested to sing *Because He Lives, I Can Face Tomorrow*. He had so much trouble just breathing that I didn't encourage him to do it; I wished I had. We did sing it at the service.

Maybe we should have made better plans for Nathan's future and more closely sought God's plan for Nathan instead of listening to those we thought knew best. Friends thought we should have a life of our own and so should Nathan, but he couldn't handle life on his own. Putting him on the strong anti-depressants in many ways added to our problems with Nathan. We can't go back to undo our mistakes and in the sovereignty of God, He allowed Nathan's life to end that way. We don't know why and we don't have to know.

Nathan taught us so much about walking with the Lord day by day. The lessons we learned could have been learned no other way. Normally children with Prader-Willi can live quite a long life, but once they develop diabetes and can't keep their weight under control, the health problems become too difficult. Most children with Prader-Willi have to be kept in supervised homes where all food is locked up. I'm glad that we kept Nathan at home. It wasn't easy but he was our son and God used Nathan to teach us that God gives good gifts and with those special gifts, He gives the wisdom and resources to raise that child for Him.

The special job that God had for Nathan was to teach his parents that God only gives good gifts and that He gives the resources and wisdom to raise that child for Him. Nathan accomplished God's goal for him in twenty-seven years. God used Nathan to shape us to be like Christ; those daily trials forced us to depend completely on God.

One area that we did prepare for the future with Nathan was a trust and guardianship.

Set up a Trust and Guardians for Your Special-Needs Child.

We had guardians chosen early for all our children in case something should happen to us, but for Nathan, we set up a trust when he was in his twenties with his brother and sister and a friend in charge. We knew that he might not have a long life but we also knew that should anything happen to us, we wanted the right situation for him. One area that we should have worked on was guiding our other children concerning Nathan's plans. Should anything have happened to us it would have been very difficult for them to handle. We should have explained to Eric and Chris how they could handle Nathan's needs if we were not able to do that. I feel that it is very important for parents to do that with whomever they choose to be in charge of the care of their special-needs child.

Wills have to be updated as the child and the parent situation changes but every family should have a will, especially a family with a child who can not live independently. Government groups are more than willing to intervene unless the parent has everything in a legal plan. As they say in advertising about will kits, if you don't want the state deciding where your estate will go, prepare a will. The same message is true for those with children who have special needs.

Set Godly Goals for Your Special-Needs Child

As I interviewed parents, I asked what their goals for their child with special needs were. Just as it was hard for us when Nathan was young, it is difficult for any parent of the child with special needs to plan 15 to 20 to 25 years ahead. Rosalie, whose youngest of seven has Downs said,

> *Our goal for four-year-old Harmony is to train her to serve God and to be a blessing to others. In order to do this, she will need good work and communication skills. We would like to train her to be as self-supporting as possible when she grows up.*

Marsha, of Missouri, said that their goals for Jessica, now thirteen, have changed. Through the 17 surgeries for her spinal bifida and hydrocephalus problems they prayed that she would live and have a faith of her own. "Now our focus is to equip her with the tools and skills necessary for her to live as self-sufficient and productive a life as is possible."

Fifteen year old, Timothy's mom said that their goal is to train him to be like Christ and to slowly become less dependent on them as he increases dependence on Christ. "We want to teach him all the life skills to handle life, get vocational training and establish him in a ministry to serve the Lord." (Timothy has a taping ministry for his church. He had a prenatal stroke that affected his whole left side.)

The goal of parents should be to raise children from complete dependence to complete independence. That isn't always possible with the special-needs child. I talked to a family in Kansas whose oldest son was oxygen deprived at birth which caused severe mental and physical disabilities. The father said, "We could have put him in a home where he probably wouldn't have lasted more than a few weeks. He lived with us until he died at age 30 and even then it was hard to give him up." Their son's disabilities were so severe that he couldn't attend school and they were told to put him in a home for the severely mentally retarded.

Since it is not always possible to prepare a special-needs child for complete independence, we need to seek God's guidance for the next best choice. God gave us that child and He has the wisdom available to know how to raise that child to their highest potential. That potential may be to teach us parents to trust the Lord through difficult circumstances. Nathan certainly did that.

Sandy of New York told of her profoundly retarded adopted daughter,

> Her loving has been what has attracted so many people to her "ministry." She has a beautiful smile and is an extremely happy child. She says, "Hi" and immediately reaches her arms for a hug. She constantly gives us the opening to tell someone about the Lord. She's our biggest blessing and God's love just shows through her.

Sheila, in North Carolina, who had two children with special needs said,

> Our goal for all our children is the same; to raise Godly children who love the Lord with all their heart. Whether they are brain surgeons, trash collectors, housewives or artists, it isn't important. We are here to "tabernacle" (fellowship) with God and not for man's pleasure. If it pleases God for one to be a doctor then we will strive for that goal but that isn't as important as our first goal.

Karen, who is visually impaired and raising a visually impaired daughter in Kansas, wrote, "...Our desire is that she reach her highest potential, and that she have a healthy attitude toward her visual limitation."

That is vital. If a child feels cheated and that God is unfair to give them all these mental and physical limitations it is often we parents who give them this attitude. Every person born has some limitation in certain areas such as color blindness, limited hearing, or weak eyes but once we see that God gives us the potential to use that limitation for good, there is no limit to what can be accomplished.

As Nellie said about her foster son with special needs,

> He's no junk. He's a real person. We want him to love himself and grow—he's God's child. Sometimes getting other relatives and friends to understand and getting them to love both C.L. and our adoptive son is very hard. Truth is, sometimes they don't. People can be rude and cruel at times. But we will always love our sweet children. We've tried to teach our children that some people may not love them and that's okay. but to always love themselves as God does.

In the January 1995, *Lookout* paper, a family with a 40-year-old son who has Down's Syndrome told how he has won many trophies in Special Olympics and how he has been able to work in a sheltered workshop. Through a literacy program, he has just recently learned to read. His mother said, "Every human being has potential in some area. Don't apologize." This man still lives with his parents.

Kathy in Texas said of her 10-year-old daughter, Sarah, who has Downs,

> My goal for Sarah is for her always to seek God's will in her life. I want her to know the fullness of Christ's love and to sacrifice to walk in His will without fear and with all wisdom. I do dream someday of her speaking in front of home schoolers or the National Down's Syndrome Congress witnessing to Christ's work in her life and how home schooling was right for her. I cannot yet see her apart from me but that is not a necessity or concern now. The Lord is sufficient—He will guide me as we go.

Kathy is right in that during those early years with a special-needs child, you either don't have time or can't plan years in advance, but in order to have your goals for your child, you need to be seeking God's plan for that child and preparing a support group to carry it out. It may be that siblings would be willing to take that responsibility but parents need to prepare them for that.

Janie in Oregon said,

> My goal for my children is in the Westminister Catechism which states "the chief end of man is to glorify God and to enjoy Him forever." This is my spiritual goal for my children, handicapped or unhandicapped. If this has been achieved by all my kids, at the end of my life, I will have considered myself blessed and truly satisfied. Practically, I would like to see my disabled children achieve physical independence and be self supporting. In Oregon, this means that parents really "hump it" because the state offers so little help. Currently I have a project going which may help solve these problems.

She continues,

> By Jonathan's very nature, if he is left in a low stimuli, "safe" (non-threatening) environment, he will perform a repetitive task for hours on end. I gave him the job of peeling, coring, and slicing forty pounds of apples and I got called away. When I returned two hours later he had processed all of them. I have a grant of food dryers from the American Harvest and help from experts concerning the food drying as a nonprofit small business. It is slow going.

Ginia, of Maryland, wrote that her goal for Andrew with Down's Syndrome is to help him reach his maximum level, love Jesus, let him enjoy life and do activities that he enjoys.

Sharon, of British Columbia, said that her goal for her adopted sons with Down's Syndrome, as well as her daughter, Florena, is that they will love God with all their hearts and seek to serve Him in every way possible.

Valerie, of Massachusetts, said that their goal for Megan is just to bring her as far as she can go.

> We don't know what her full potential is, but we want to help her reach it. And I think what is most important to me is that she learn without a doubt that Jesus loves her and that she come to love and accept Him as her Savior.

Jackie, of Colorado, wrote,

> Our main focus of course is to bring all our children to the saving knowledge of Jesus Christ, and to be with each one in heaven. Our goal

for Christopher is for him to achieve to the height of his ability in anything he has a bent towards. So far we haven't seen only one thing he wants to pursue. We just try and provide many opportunities and activities so he can find something he loves. For us, at his age, we don't know all he can reach for. Only God and time will tell.

Nellie, of Oklahoma, said that her goal for C.L. "Is her happiness and her independence, at least to her ability."

Phil and Linda, of Minnesota, wrote that their main purpose for their adopted son was to discover and prepare him for God's purpose for his life. "Our goal for him is that he would glorify God and enjoy Him forever."

Laura, of Michigan, said, "I want Gideon to be all God wants him to be. I don't want to force him or push him too hard. I want him to keep his openness and love for people."

Mary of Indiana wrote that her main goal for Gary was, "A Godly Character."

Lane's mother, Carol, of Kansas said,

This has to be the most confusing area right now for me. I am totally baffled. Each special-needs child I know has such a variety of needs that there are no specific examples to look at to really help. I hope that Lane can be as independent as possible for him in the future, but what the realities of that statement are, I simply do not know at this time. We are starting to check into the various types of living facilities for adults and trying to see our son's needs, but it is very hard to think of a semi-dependent person relying on people you don't know to take care of him. This will take a lot of searching yet. Lane's limited mental understanding makes it nearly impossible to discuss his desires for the future. One time when I asked him about living somewhere else or at home, he said, "Want to live with Mom." Probably my biggest concern is finding a safe place where the care-givers can be trusted.

Jean, of Kansas, answered the question of potential for Tyler with,

Our hope is that he will be able to function normally and by the time he is in high school he could go without any help all day. We would like for him to go to college to learn a trade and be an asset to the world. Knowing that he can read now is a beginning. We want him to try hard and become the best and his skills develop so he can go on to college.

Terry and Robert of Maryland, told me that their goal for adopted Stephen is,

> *Spiritually, to make sure to give him the opportunity to understand the saving grace of God that is available through Jesus and are praying that he will one day come to know Christ as his personal Savior. To not set any predetermined limits on what he can do in the area of academics, social skills, physical skills etc. and give him the opportunities, education and training that he needs to learn all that he is capable of.*

Debbie, of Kansas, wrote that their focus for all their children is, "to raise them, as best we can, to be what the Lord God wants them to be. Overall, we want Travis to try his best, to do his best and to glorify God."

Su of Wisconsin said that their goal for Ben is to become independent, a part of "society" but mostly to fulfill *God's* plan for his life. Ben has fulfilled much of that goal already.

Ellen of Kansas said of 25-year-old Becky, "She has potential of being a household helper, mailing helper and perhaps helper in a restaurant."

Janice, of Kansas, said "God's desire is that I train these children to the fullest potential that He has for them. God focuses on the heart, not on the outward or mental ability of any child."

Selena, of Kansas, answered the question of her main focus for Stephanie with, "Just to help her become the most she can be and do the most that she can and not to limit her by my lack of vision or the professional's predictions."

Mary Ann, of Kansas, said that her main goal for her son was that he get at least a high school diploma so he could go on if he wants to for college courses. He did do that by the time he was just over sixteen with her home educating him from seventh grade.

A mother of Maryland wrote, "Our goal for our son is that he would do his best to God's glory, that he grow in the Lord, that he be able to function in society and that he become self-sufficient to the best of his ability."

The goals for the future of the special-needs child may be somewhat different than normal children but as several mothers mentioned they wanted their children to glorify God and to become all that God had for them. If a parent accomplishes that, the child will be a useful vessel for God. Every child needs to know they have worth, and true worth comes from knowing God, and that God has a special job just for them; understanding that they have a future in heaven with Him, where they will no longer have all the mental and physical problems. He will give them hope during the difficult times.

CHAPTER FOURTEEN
A Word To the Wise

Proverbs 9:10
"The fear of God is the beginning of wisdom."

Parents Never Stop Learning

Those first six weeks after Nathan's death were difficult. We knew that he was with the Lord and in that knowledge we could rejoice. It says in I Thessalonians 4:13 "But I do not want you to be ignorant, brethren, concerning those who have fallen asleep, *lest you sorrow as others who have no hope.*" He didn't say we wouldn't sorrow or grieve but it is a different kind of grieving.

Memorial weekend, seven weeks after Nathan's death, my brother-in-law called to say that he had placed a mum plant on Nathan's grave. He wanted me to bring it home to plant in the yard. I've never been one to visit cemeteries so it was difficult to drive to Nathan's grave especially since the day was so dreary and cloudy. I found the grave beside my mother's grave and the beautiful little mum of the brightest yellow. As I drove home crying, I turned on the Christian radio station to hear the most beautiful piano solo of *To God Be the Glory.* While it played, a sunbeam slid out from under the clouds. I felt as if God was reminding me that He was caring for Nathan now. I could trust Him with knowing that I would see Nathan again.

Ellis and I kept busy with our regular routine; I planted a garden even though my heart wasn't in it. Nathan's little puppy, which I had tried to give to our oldest son, became wonderful company for both of us. You can't feel sorry for yourself with a little puppy jumping all over you. We still took the long walks that had refreshed us through other trials. After almost six weeks, Ellis mentioned, "You know I think we are beginning to heal from the grieving."

Through all the 27 years of raising and training Nathan, *he taught us* much on the practical application of Biblical principles:

1. That God designs every person from conception so we can thank God

for our special-needs child no matter how mentally or physically impaired they may be.

2. God gives parents the responsibility and wisdom to raise children and especially for the special-needs child. No one will care for that child like a parent. He has the resources parents need. We only have to ask, seek and knock.

3. God can give parents the wisdom to discern between learning disabilities or character deficits. Parents far excel any professional in the educational or medical field in knowing and understanding their own children.

4. All children and especially the special-needs child should not be pampered but pushed to develop to their highest ability or they will not become the useful vessels God can use.

5. God has given parents the responsibility of educating their children. We will answer to God for what we did with that responsibility. May He say, "Well done thou good and faithful servant."

6. God looks at the heart, not mental ability, concerning spiritual aptitude. That is true for all of us. We can thank God for that truth.

7. The safest environment to learn social abilities is the home where they are taught in a loving atmosphere. No matter what the special need, they need to learn proper manners and behavior so that they are a joy to all people and in all situations they encounter.

8. Parents can have the satisfaction in a job well done when they have followed Biblical principles in raising their child with special needs or we reap what we sow by our neglect.

9. Normal children need to be given special training and love to adjust to the needs of a special-needs sibling as well as the knowledge that they are just as important to the parents as their special-needs sibling.

10. Parents must allow time for themselves and their own relationship or unresolved problems will pull them apart.

11. Parents should make plans for the future of the special-needs child to be assured that their goals will be met by whoever is the caregiver/guardian.

Other Parents Have Succeeded with Special-Needs Kids

Each of the parents that I interviewed were asked what advice they would give other parents. They had excellent ideas—some were ones that hadn't occurred to me. They would have helped during the time we were struggling with Nathan's problems. Here is their advice:

Mary Ann of Kansas, who started home schooling their youngest in the seventh grade:

> *Realize that it takes a lot of work and effort, but the end results for me and him <u>were worth</u> the effort and time it took. Even though some days I sure wondered <u>why</u> did I do this? But I ended up with a child who reads and writes and I hope maybe will go to Kansas Technological Institute for some computer courses later.*

Mary of Indiana said, "The best advice I can share with other special-needs families is to trust God. He will show you what is best for your child. Spend much time in prayer for each of your children."

Selena of Kansas said,

> *Read everything you can read, learn all you can learn. Ask questions until people are sick of you. Pray and enlist the prayers of a regular prayer group. Ask for their prayers and give them an update and the praises. I listen and observe Stephanie and God shows me specifically things I need to know.*
>
> *As right as home schooling has been for our family, I would not be so brash as to say it is a cure-all for everyone. It requires tremendous commitment by both parents. Both parents must agree and the mother must be prepared to take on a full time job with no paycheck at the end of the week. Write down your reasons and/or goals as you first begin to home school. It may only be reasons at first. Many home school to meet a child's special need, or because we believe God is directing that way, or for religious convictions or whatever. When frustrated and overwhelmed, a normal reaction is to quit, thinking we made the wrong choice. Satan would like for you to believe you made the wrong choice. In reality, when you go back over your reasons/goals perhaps your emotions and feelings have changed but your goals have not. It is a tough job so you need to have God to draw on. Gradually the longer you are in home schooling and as other people observe your children the more supportive they become.*

Tammy in Kansas said, "Find out the educational problem of your child and try working with him. It can't hurt."

A mother in Maryland said that home schooling had caused the family to form a tight bond. Talking about the situation had helped them. She said,

> For our son, his self-esteem was getting destroyed in school. He felt he couldn't compete with the other children. He doesn't have to compete at home. He can finish a unit when he understands it and not when the class moves on. This makes him feel much more positive. He is actually starting to read just for fun. "...and your strength will equal your days." Deuteronomy 33:25b.

Sharon from British Columbia who home schools two sons with Downs along with her daughter said,

> It is a lot of hard work having special-needs children and it can be very frustrating and trying but if we hang in there and look towards the final goal that's what is important. All things work together for good for those that love the Lord! God bless you.

Ellen from Kansas whose youngest daughter has Downs and is now 26 years, said,

> Indeed God doesn't make junk! However, we don't sometimes see that right away and our problem is to accept and love our "special" child as He does. So if others, like myself during the first weeks after Becky's birth, wrestle with God over having given them such a child, we need to cast our burden of resentment and anger on Him; we can't carry this burden, only He can and will (Psalm 55:22) Thank God for all joys, large and small. Don't give in to self pity or to anger at "normal" people who don't understand. Rest in Him.

Jean of Kansas with an autistic son said,

> Don't give up and keep trying and keep working with the professionals. If one doctor doesn't give you the help you need or one teacher doesn't give the help you need, keep trying. You must have a strong faith in God. When all else fails our faith in God has brought us through. Church helps, we try to teach a lot about God and Jesus at home. I want Tyler to know that if no one likes him or accepts him that God and Jesus

are there for him. We talk a lot about that.

Terry and Robert's advice from Maryland was, "Always look at the child as an individual." Terry said,

> I saw written somewhere, to remember that they are children _with_ Down's Syndrome (or with Cerebral Palsy or whatever) and not as Down's Syndrome children. Never try to teach them something because you have been told or always assumed, they could not learn that. Give them opportunities to succeed.

Fay in North Carolina said,

> The only things I can say is to love your special-needs child unconditionally. To accept them for who they are and what they can do and work with them to help them improve their situation as much as possible. I feel that home schooling has been best for Heather because of the experience we have had with our other children…

From Kansas, Debbie's advice was,

> The best advice I could give to any parents of a child with special needs would be to pray and to lift up your child/children daily (all your children, not just special-needs ones). Prayer has been healing Travis of his disability. Also don't give up; ask God for guidance and wisdom and direction, giving thanks for that special child.

Evelyn from Kansas said,

> Love and accept your child. Help your child become independent early in life. Teach him/her how to cook, clean house and manage for himself/herself. Always remember to treat your child with love and respect. Above all, have patience. It may take several attempts for your child to learn how to do something. Don't give up on your child.
> I keep thinking that God created Kari (now 24) for a specific purpose. He did not make a mistake. It wasn't my fault. I need to constantly be in prayer so I can help Kari reach her full God-given potential.

Cindy, whose son has Prader-Willi Syndrome in Kansas said,

> One of the areas that has bothered me the most is looking at the future and being afraid of it and what's out there and what's to come. I think looking back on it, that I missed some real special times that I could have had if I had been looking at the moment rather than worrying about what is ahead. It was not something to fear but to look at where we are at this time. He was such a happy baby with this incredible disposition and still is except for the times when he has these little temper tantrums. If I could just have enjoyed those times rather than worrying about, "why is my child this way?" The fear of the unknown is something I would like to help others overcome.

Janice of Kansas, home educating two children with special needs, said,

> There is the commitment of time and patience. It really is time consuming! You will be responsible for educational, emotional, spiritual and physical need. Parents should also remember that progress is slow and almost immeasureable at times. So don't let yourself get discouraged.

From Kansas, Verna's advice to parents was,

> Depend on the child with special needs; don't treat them different than your other children. Expect them to do what the others do. Push to the upper limit but watch for that fine line to where you frustrate them. It is not helpful to label them educationally. Teach them that if first they don't succeed, try again.

Ginia of Maryland said,

> Each child, family, and parent is different so what might apply to us may not apply to them. But one thing that always works for me is to trust what *I* feel is right because I believe and I feel it for a reason. Many people, family, teachers, doctors, etc. told me to do many different things "for Andrew" but I didn't feel right about them so I stuck to "Andrew" and what I felt and it always was best. I feel I was listening to God.

Another mother in Kansas gave this advice:

> Look to experienced home schoolers for advice. There were about three families who started about the same time we did with special-needs children. We had physical, speech, and occupational therapy at the

Institute of Logopedics for our daughter. Insurance paid for that. She was in a developmental preschool (not public) until she was five so she received therapy. Through five to eight, she received no therapy. Now we are doing most of her therapy at home. We do aerobics three or four times a week. Some hospitals will develop home programs if you can't afford their programs. Sometimes insurance will pay for the hospital program. You need to tell them this is reasonable and necessary.

Carol in Kansas, whose 16 year old son has multiple handicaps, said,

Each child's needs are so different that it is hard to be specific. Love them, teach them, accept them, love them some more. Find out as much as you can about their special needs. There are many resources available and we need to tap into them. This is one area I did not take advantage of the first few years. I guess we were just surviving.

Valerie in Massachusetts said,

To me home schooling is a way of life, a lifestyle. There are opportunities to learn through every aspect of life. We learn through activities of daily living, through regular errands in the community, through our church activities and our special excursions to museums, the Aquarium, etc. We love field trips! I find that through home schooling I'm learning so much!

In the beginning I was a bit nervous about everything. Besides wanting to do everything perfectly, I was nervous about what people would say. Now I'm more confident and relaxed. I'm not afraid of people's reactions—home schooling is our decision and we are following it because this is what God wants for us. I love educating people about home schooling, especially because some people have misconceptions about it and are surprised when they learn the truth.

Karen from Kansas gives this advice:

a. *Get help as soon as possible. Early intervention has made all the difference in our lives. And if you don't get what you think you need, keep asking. Be persistent. Don't give up.*

b. *Talk, talk, talk. Talk about your feelings, interact with your child, explain what is happening to him/or her in language he/she can understand.*

c. *Treat your child as a whole person.* We chose to take the risk of having children with possible vision difficulties because we saw what God has done in my life; that even though life has been tough at times, life is more than a pair of dysfunctional eyeballs. Even if your child has many handicaps, he/she has something unique to offer the world.

d. *Be encouraging and thankful.* Always encourage your child no matter how small the progress. Be sure to thank the helpers that come your way. The system will be a lot more willing to work with you if they see that you are willing to work with them. Thank you notes sprinkled here and there work wonders. But do it genuinely, not for selfish gain.

e. *Keep a balanced approach.* It is sometimes easy to pour oneself into the needs of the handicapped child and forget the rest of the family or your own needs. Don't be afraid to ask for outside help if you need a break. You will be more effective if you do.

Marilyn of Pennsylvania gave this list:

1. *Accept God's design for your child.*
2. *Help him/her develop all that God has equipped him to do.*
3. *Develop a spirit of good self-worth.*
4. *Don't allow roots of bitterness in you or the child.*
5. *Get encouragement and help if needed.*
6. *Develop a "life's" message testimony "with" your child to see God's design in their lives.*
7. *Encourage dependence on God and independence on you.*

Terry and Marsha of Missouri gave this advice:

Keep God as your guide in every situation. It's too hard by yourself. Get past the emotional pain of the situation and move to acceptance. See your child as God sees them. Believe in yourself and the decisions you make, especially when others criticize you. You're the one that has to live with the results of your decisions, not them. Don't take the advice of those that are being negative. Only consider the advice of those that love you unconditionally without judgment. Be an advocate for your child so that they can have all the tools and opportunities they need to develop all the abilities they have.

Encourage them to try and allow them to succeed or fail on their own. Be close by for support. Teach your child to be a problem solver, because new situations will always come up. Teach your child to value themselves, by teaching that God values them, and by your words and actions, that you value them. There is much of the world that will not value them. Talk to your child about everything, honestly, even if you aren't sure they understand. If they're old enough to ask about something, they're old enough to hear the truth. If you don't talk to them about something now, or aren't honest with them about it, they won't ask you later. They'll ask someone else.

Be prepared to be rejected by your family, friends, and church. This is not a popularity contest. If you choose to take the journey of caring for a special-needs child, you have to put your child first. Your family, friends, and church may not understand. But remember, if they don't love you and support you now, they really didn't care about you before. God will give you the love and support you need Himself, and through people you meet in the years to come. Also be prepared to not get understanding from your co-workers or your boss. There may be times you will change jobs, by your choice or theirs, because of misunderstandings over needing time off for your child's care or over insurance issues.

Pick your battles carefully. Assess the cost before you start a legal battle, not just financially but also psychologically and emotionally. If it's a medical legal battle, and your child will need future care, other doctors may not be willing to help. If your child might lose, even if you win the fight, don't start the fight. God will right the wrongs for you. Know when to walk away, even if you know you're right. Put a degree of faith in your doctors but remember they are also human. Stay in control of the medical decisions by asking a lot of questions, studying the medical procedures to be done and thinking about what it will be like to live with the outcome of their medical treatments. Talk to parents of other children that have the same procedures done, but again, remember not to listen to those that are always negative. The doctors know the procedures but they don't personally know what it's like to live with the results in everyday life.

Marsha and Terry continue,

> *Being a parent of a special-needs child has its advantages. It becomes much easier to see which people really care and which ones don't. We've all heard that it's better to give than to receive. Don't be afraid to receive from others, or they'll never know the joy of giving. This could be a time when you'll need to receive more than you can give. Be thankful and gracious in receiving. It's hard to get joy out of giving to someone who doesn't appreciate the gift. But remember, don't be afraid to say "no" if you're not sure that the motivation of the giver is pure. Gifts that aren't given unconditionally aren't gifts; they're loans. And those loans will be recalled at the very worst times.*
>
> *Don't be afraid to try new things, even if everyone else says it won't work. Weigh the risks and prayerfully seek God. If He says, "don't do it," don't. If God says "do it," then do it. Know that God has a <u>daily</u> plan for your child's life, just as He does for yours. Long term plans are great to have, but don't let the long term overshadow what God can do in your life <u>today</u>. Don't get in the way of God working in the lives of others, <u>through your child</u>. You have been given a great gift in your special-needs child. With great gifts come great responsibilities.*

Jackie from Colorado wrote:

> *I would tell parents of special-needs or any child for that matter, if they're considering home schooling to sit back and take evaluation. Evaluate how satisfied they are with what their children are learning or what potential of learning they have in school. Evaluate their time. I <u>do not</u> believe patience is something to evaluate. This is a character trait that needs to be developed in <u>all</u> parents. That is a lame excuse not to home school. They need to consider all factors. And not to home school because they are pressured or because it's the latest fad but to really look at their own family situation.*

Sheila of North Carolina wrote: "Pray, persevere. Accept the challenge. You know your child better than anyone else! God willing, you can help your child be or do what God has planned."

Sandy in New York gave this advice:

> *You know your child better than anyone else does, and God just*

never makes mistakes in how your child was born or who he was placed with. We never question God when we like His ideas or His commands, but we have a tendency to always ask "why?" when we don't like what He's said. Someone told me once to never buy a dress on sale just because it was on sale. If you wouldn't buy it for the full price, don't buy it for the sale. That reminds me of our special kids. Why consider home schooling for them when the world more and more looks at them as just worth a sale price? Because I'd pay full price for my special child any day. God made her perfect in His sight.

Linda from Minnesota said,

<u>Each</u> of us is special in God's sight. God supplies and multiplies resources. He is able to do exceedingly abundantly above all we ask or think. In serving others, we ourselves are watered. Learn what you need to know to be a skilled advocate for your child, but then let go and let God...Keep your search for information very broad. Continuing in the Word of God builds faith and develops spiritual discernment. Turn over every stone. Learn to be a gleaner. Eat the fish and spit out the bones.

Jane of Oregon wrote,

This may seem a little simplistic, but in addition to all the other counsel interwoven in my other responses, I have one piece of advice. This is drawn from years of experience dealing with lots of families in support groups. To build a healthy family life, if your marriage is strong and if your handicapped child is your first one, have another baby. Of course, if there is a legitimate genetic scare; you may choose to adopt, but a healthy child brings joy and support into a family. On the cold practical side, another child will be there for your handicapped child when the Lord has called you home, but that is just a perk, not a main reason. Mostly you need to share your focus. It is very easy to become so wrapped up in your handicapped child that you both lose out and another child is a great solution to the problem.

Su of Wisconsin said,

Find his/her special qualities—they are there! <u>Major</u> in them. (We formed the <u>whole</u> curriculum around his interests and gifts. We used job shadows, apprenticeships and volunteer programs) Find what imbal-

ances (Biochemistry) are in your child. There are professionals who can help with this. Ben never took insulin or any medications. He has used water, diet and some supplements.

Laura of Michigan wrote,

> *My advice would be to seek God. Parents get too caught up in trying to please the professionals, the grandparents, and even themselves. Let the child be who God made him to be. Encourage him in the gifts and talents he was blessed with. Example: our son hates to color, holding pencils or crayons is hard for him because of limited rotation in his arm. We're not going to push him to be an artist or an author. He loves music and can play his keyboard any time. We sing a lot. We play different styles of music. We have guitars, bongos, bells, etc. Also, be firm in your belief that God has blessed you with a joyful responsibility. Don't allow others to drag you down. You're doing the best you can.*

These parents have learned so many valuable lessons working with their special-needs children. They are exceeding my knowledge and experience because they are in the "thick of the battle" right now. If anything in this book is helpful, it has to come from the lessons that God taught us through some demanding experiences. God will give you the same strength, wisdom and courage.

Sources of Help for Parents of Special-Needs Children

Prader-Willi Syndrome Assoc. headquarters at 2510 S. Brentwood Blvd., Suite 220, St Louis, Missouri 63144, Phone 800-926-4797.

For Down's Syndrome: The Michael Fund #721, 400 Penn Center Blvd., Pittsburg, Pennsylvania 15235.

A group that helps churches mainstream students with disabilities in Sunday School, VBS and worship services is: Christian Church Foundation for the Handicapped (CCFH). Write Dr. Jim Pierson, P.O. Box 6869, Knoxville, Tennessee 37940, Phone 615-579-0883; fax requests 616-579-0942.

Most other SN problems also have a national headquarters for information.

Another good resource for all special needs is: *NATHHAN Magazine*, 5383 Alpine Road SE, Olalla Washington 98359. Phone or fax 206-857-4257. They publish a quarterly magazine to encourage, inform, educate and provide resources for home-educating children with special needs. They suggest $25 for a one year membership which gives you use of their lending library.

JAF Ministries (Joni and Friends) has a monthly newsletter accelerating Christian ministry in the disability community. Their address is P.O. Box 3333, Agoura Hills, CA 91301. Phone: 818-707-5664; Fax 818-707-2391; TDD: 818-707-9709; E-Mail: 102704.3130@compuserve.com

Resource Material for Special-Needs Children:

Selena Book of Abilene, Kansas supplied this list. She said that she would be glad to talk to any parent. Her address is: 1019 2000 Ave., Abilene, Kansas 67410. Phone: 913-263-7545.

Turnabout Children by Mary MacCracken (very good)

A Parents Guide to Learning Disabilities by Johanna Fisher (very good)

Helping Children Overcome Learning Disabilities by Jerome Rosner (Selena's favorite)

Preparing for Adolescence by James Dobson (very good)

Parenting Isn't for Cowards by James Dobson (very good)

Learners-Slow by Peter Bell

Home is a Learning Place by Helen Ginandes Weiss

Verbal Learning and Retention by John Fry Hall

Learning by Doing by Carlos Clinton Crawford

Montessori: Prescription for Children by Reginald Calvert Orem

Human Characteristics and School Learning by Benjamin Samuel Bloom

How Children Learn by John Holt

RIF Guide to Encouraging Young Readers by Reading is Fundamental

Underachievers by Benjamin Fine

On Helping the Dyslexic Child by T.R. Miles

Basic Teaching for Slow Learners by Peter Ball

Alphabetical Listing of References

"Autistic...or just shy?" Dr. Thomas Sowell, *Forbes*, August 1, 1994

Children With Disabilities a Medical Primer by Dr. Mark Batshaw and Yvonne M. Perret, MA MSW, LCSW, Paul H. Brookes Publishing, Baltimore Maryland 21285. 1992

Christian Home Educators of California, P.O. Box 28644 Santa Ana, CA 92799, from a special brochure prepared to answer common questions relating to home education.

Dramatized Bible stories can be ordered from Bible in Living Sound, Box 234, Nordland, Washington 98358. Phone: 1-800-634-0234, Pacific time 9-5. They are called, *The Bible In Living Sound*. They are now on cassette tapes.

First Reader System, Inc. P.O. Box 495 Alton, Illinois 62002. Phone 618-462-8622. Orders and Inquiries 800-700-5228. There are other readers using the phonics method. This is one with which I am familiar.

Home School Legal Defense Association, P.O. Box 159, Peaonia Springs, Virginia 22129. Phone 703-388-2733.

Inside American Education by Thomas Sowell 1993. The Free Press A Division of Macmillan, Inc. 866 Third Ave., New York, New York 10022.

Let's Hide the Word Gloria Gaither and Shirley Dobson. Published by Word Publishing, Dallas, TX 1994. This can be purchased from any Christian bookstore in paperback.

May's Boy, Shirlee Monty, (Thomas Nelson Publishers, Nashville, 1981)

Phyllis Schlafly Report 1994. You may subscribe to her monthly letter for $20 a year from: Eagle Forum Trust Fund, Box 618, Alton, Illinois 62202. This is excellent material from a Christian lawyer and teacher.

Preparing for Adolescence by Dr. James Dobson, 1978 by Vision House Publishers, Santa Anna, CA 92705.

The Gifts They Bring by Pearl Buck, John Day Company 1965

The Teaching Home, July/Aug 1994, Guest Editorial, "Warning to Home Schoolers!" P.O. Box 12311, Portland, OR 97230.

What About Their Peer Relationships by Paul E. White, Ph.D., 1994 Published by Family Resources, 9130 Barron, Wichita, KS 67207.

About the Authors

Ellis and Donna Adee have been leaders and teachers in their small church in Minneapolis, Kansas for almost 40 years. God has used them to teach Bible studies in homes within 50 miles of their farm during the last 30 years. They still continue to farm wheat and milo but have cut back in acreage to allow more time for ministry and their grandchildren.

Donna has been a leader of Mothers and Others, a community-wide group, since it started in 1986. Both Donna and Ellis are leaders in the AWANA children's club at their church.

Donna's articles have been published in *Mature Living, Power for Living,* the *Prader- Willi Assoc. Newsletter* as well as the *NATHHAN* magazine for parents of/with special needs children. Several of her humorous stories have appeared in farm magazines.

Their oldest son, Eric, a plant pathologist, is a supervisor of a research farm for the University of Illinois. His wife, Shelly, also a plant pathologist, has chosen to be a stay-at-home mom with their son, Daniel.

Their daughter, Chris, with a degree in horticulture, is raising three children and home educating the two oldest at this time. She and her family live near Tonganoxie, Kansas where her husband, Kelly, teaches math in the public high school, coaches track and cross country and runs a landscaping business.

FAIRFIELD MS/HS MEDIA CENTER
16115 S. Langdon Rd.
Langdon, Kansas 67583